For Hilda

Till a' the seas gang dry, my dear,
  And the rocks melt wi' the sun!
And I will luve thee still, my dear,
  While the sands o' life shall run.

Robert Burns

Contents

Introduction

The essays presented in this short book range across several areas of thought and action: philosophy, politics, general culture, morality, science, religion and art. Intermittently they discuss the lives and work of various figures past and present, and at various points they highlight aspects of Scottish intellectual life and social culture. In these respects they may remind some readers of a once strong tradition of philosophical reflection on human manners, opinions and practices. That tradition was well represented among philosophers in Britain, in Europe and in North America; but it had special associations with Scotland in the period of its Enlightenment and in the century that succeeded it, when philosophy was thought to be a mode of general understanding of matters of broad interest among thinking people. To some extent the role of this kind of reflection has passed to popularisers of history and science. This has brought different perspectives to bear but it has also meant that a distinctive kind of analysis and argument has moved to the margins. To some extent philosophers have been to blame for failing to take their place in the public space, and for narrowing the range and increasing the technicality of their intellectual enquiries. Of late, however, there seems to be a recognition on the part of a few that they need to re-enter the general forum, and some have done so to good effect. I hope that others will follow where they have led.

What unites these reflections is an interest, indeed a preoccupation with questions of meaning, value and understanding. Deep down in human kind and never far from the

surface of serious human activities lies a desire for fulfilment. That desire has several aspects including cognitive,
emotional and practical ones. In one or another way we seek
meaning in the world around us while also trying to make
sense of our own lives and of the human condition more
generally. Sometimes the particularities and the details of
immediate concerns obscure the fact that what are at issue
are larger questions concerning the content and status of
morality, the character of community, the purposes of society, the role of the arts, the possibilities of transcendence,
and similarly fundamental matters.

These essays are deliberately short, and cover a wide
range of topics. Their aim is to prompt readers to think
about the issues for themselves, in the hope that what is
written may engage interest, inform, guide, and occasionally entertain. While they do proceed according to a plan
they can be read independently and out of sequence. They
propose no single thesis but do offer, and try to defend, a
picture of the human condition as framed by and respon-
sive to objective orders of reason and value.

John Haldane
St Andrews

Acknowledgements

I am grateful to Anthony Freeman, Peter Sampson, and Gladys Sweeney who each in different ways contributed to the preparation of this volume.

Most of the material presented here originates in whole or in part in articles first published in a range of newspapers and journals, and in one case in a radio broadcast. All have been modified to some degree. The original sources are as follows:

1. 'The search for meaning' first appeared as 'The Herald Essay: It is part of the human form of life to deliberate and act in accord with reasons' in *The Herald*, 15 May 1999.

2. 'Making sense of the universe' is a shortened version of an essay entitled 'Scotland's Gift: Philosophy, Theology, and the Gifford Lectures' published in *Theology Today*, January 2007.

3. 'Plain talk and common sense philosophy', first appeared as 'On Common Sense' in *The Scottish Review*, Autumn 2002. It was based on the script of a talk 'A short History of Common Sense' broadcast on BBC Radio 3 during the 2002 Edinburgh Festival.

4. 'Making sense of society' derives from 'The Herald Essay: The most noble liberalism is one tolerant of difference, not indifferent to morals, *The Herald*, 24 October 1998.

5. 'A disuniting kingdom' draws material from 'The Celtic Conversion of England', *The Times*, 22 July 1997, and 'Union Flagging', *The Tablet*, 20 January 2007.

6. 'Making sense of humanity' expands upon 'Adam, Apes and Angels' from *The Herald*, 17 January 1998.

7. 'Respecting life: ethics and embryos' combines material from 'In the Defence of Life', *The Chronicle*, 12 March 1996, and 'An Ethical Dilemma', *Life and Work*, November 2006.

8. 'Respecting life: ethics and waging war' draws from 'Examining the Justice of War', *Humanitas*, April 2003.

9. 'A union of communities' combines 'Wrong to look down our noses at America' and 'Divided America still the united states' *The Scotsman* 17 March and 28 November 2006.

10. 'Moral tales' first appeared as 'Toying with our morals' in *Night & Day* (*Mail on Sunday* magazine) 6 February 2000.

11. 'Making sense of evil' is a longer version of an article that appeared as 'Devilish conceit' in *Critique* (*The Scotsman* arts and culture magazine) 1 April 2006.

12. 'Fiction's enigma variations' is based on an article of the same title published in *The Scotsman*, 18 May 2006 and reprinted in the *John Buchan Journal*, Spring 2006.

13. 'Yarn spinning and soul making' derives from 'John Buchan: A Scottish Philosopher Reflects', *John Buchan Journal*, Autumn 1998.

14. 'Taking thought seriously' combines material from 'Any questions except those that are philosophical' and 'Brilliant battler in defence of human dignity' from *The Scotsman*, 17 and 19 June 2006.

15. 'Making sense of religion' first appeared as 'Opiate of the Philosophers' in *Commonweal*, 10 March 2006.

16. 'Arguing over God' is a version of 'In the Crossfire' from *The Tablet*, 24 November, 2007.

17. 'Making sense of art and science' derives from a talk given in the Edinburgh Festival in 1997 under the auspices of the Demarco European Art Foundation.

18. 'Making sense of nature' draws from 'Back to the Land', *Art Monthly*, June 1999, and 'Art's Natural Revolutionary', *The Scotsman*, 29 June 2007.

19. 'Finding meaning in enchantment' originated as 'A Poet of the Enchanted World' published in *Modern Painters*, Spring 2002.

One

The Search for Meaning

When philosophers discuss philosophy they usually do so for the interest of other philosophers. That is understandable. Philosophy is an academic discipline with questions to answer and methods for dealing with them. It also has a two and a half thousand year old history with the years marked by the works of great figures. Anyone who wishes to practise seriously as a philosopher has to be familiar with the established questions, methods and texts. At the same time, however, philosophy is too important for its fruits only to be distributed among professionals. Almost every intelligent person will ask themselves about the origins of the universe, the meaning of life, the existence of God, the possibility of an after-life, the nature of good and bad, and so on. These are unmistakably philosophical questions and philosophers should try to relate their own concentrated efforts at answering them to the loosely structured reflections of people in general.

The historical meaning of the term philosophy is love of wisdom (*philo-sophia*). Beginning in the third century BC the Stoics distinguished between 'philosophy' and 'discourse about philosophy'. The first concerns living wisely, recognising things for what they are, appreciating the opportunities and limitations that life offers and dealing justly with others—knowing well and acting well. 'Discourse about philosophy', by contrast, aims to understand the funda-

1

mental concepts and principles of natural science, logic and ethics. Stoics and members of the other ancient schools engaged in such abstract discourse; but their main concern was to devise ways of living that embody wisdom and the love of it—*philosophies*. So it was with Augustine in the 5th century and with Descartes in the 17th. Yet present-day philosophers are for the most part only interested in technical discourse: philosophical theories rather than philosophical life. This restriction is a great mistake, I believe, and is due to the strong influence of scientific thought whose main concern is the physical composition of the world.

Marx wrote that 'the various philosophers have only interpreted the world differently; what matters is to change it'. In this he was seeing a truth but through a distorting lens. It is important to understand the nature of reality but it is also necessary—and humanly speaking more important—to know how to live well. It is not part of the philosopher's vocation to change the world but it may well be part of his duty to change himself. And when those who are not philosophers periodically adopt a philosophical stance they too must ask how they should live.

Philosophy must make contact with the ancient aims of becoming wise and virtuous. Christian authors such as Augustine developed the idea of original sin to explain the darkening of the intellect and the disturbance of the passions. They suggested that such flaws make it difficult for us to achieve enlightenment, but they had no doubt as to the objective value of wisdom or virtue, or of their necessity for living a meaningful life. Indeed there has been agreement upon this necessity throughout the first two thousand years of philosophy.

Currently, though, there are some who reject this entire tradition as resting on false (or even incoherent) assumptions. If these radical and subversive critics are right, then searching for meaning in life is like hunting for unicorns—both are pointless activities based on empty myths. Yet, reflective people continue to ask questions about whether their lives, or life in general, has meaning. Like the ancients, the medievals and the moderns, I take these questions very seriously, much more seriously than I take the declarations of nihilism. But in order to refute the claims of the subversive critics one must first understand them.

According to these radicals we have rightly lost confidence in the values that we once shared; in the institutions of society and in intellectual, moral, aesthetic and spiritual authority — in short the familiar package of elements that constitute a fairly stable social and cultural order. The critics' challenging and unsettling thought is that we have left all that behind us and are now in circumstances of profound uncertainty. Sometimes this is expressed in terms of the imagery of fracture and disintegration: fragmentation of reason, fragmentation of public culture and a resulting confusion of perspectives. We find ourselves in what some like to describe as a 'postmodern condition', one in which the possibility of public discussion is undermined by apparently ineliminable features of contemporary thought: the absence of values or extensive and irresolvable disagreement about them.

Put another way, we have lost and cannot any longer construct a human philosophy, an account of our nature that has extensive implications for the conduct of individual and social life; a way of thinking about what we are which is directly relevant to how we ought to live. There are narrowly drawn, rich and powerful philosophies, and there are looser, broader more encompassing philosophies. One kind is the religious world view offered by Christianity. Marxism is another obvious instance. Liberalism also counts in this reckoning as a type of philosophy. Certainly, its post-modern critics regard traditional liberalism as part of the philosophical and ideological history of the West, and view it as rooted in untenable rationalistic ideas.

There are several grounds on which systems of value and meaning have come to be rejected. One claim is that ways of thinking that have dominated western culture for the last two and a half millennia conceive of the course of human history as having some kind of significance or value (and often as ascending or declining). Obvious instances of this are ideas of sacred history; for example, the 'developmental' view found in Hebrew scripture and taken up and extended by Christianity. Thus, Augustine thinks in terms of the sequence of creation, fall, incarnation, atonement, redemption and so on. Likewise we can see a de-Christianised version of the flow of events in nineteenth century thinkers who interpret the human condition in terms of an intellectual, cultural, or political narrative. Postmodern critics contend that we simply cannot deceive ourselves into thinking that human history has any kind of significance, providing clues as to what we are and how we ought to live.

A related criticism insists that there is nothing to look to save the facts laid bare by science; and mindful of subjectivity, there may not even be this. At best there is a continuing process of chemico-physical interaction between bits of matter. Any effort to find a perspective that goes beyond this is impossible, be it the transcendental viewpoints of religion or of pure reason. Even the latter is undermined by the idea that science and social criticism have taught us that there is only a valueless material universe to which human imagination has added the myths of rationality.

A third criticism rejects attempts to discover defining features of human nature. Such efforts have taken various forms including the theories of eighteenth century Scottish thinkers. While these authors rejected pure rationalism in favour of observation and conjecture, they nonetheless supposed that human nature may be universal, and that on this basis a theory of value might be advanced. Unsurprisingly, postmodern critics argue that this retains the form of untenable essentialism, assuming an objective 'human nature' by which one might understand individuals and society.

A final criticism is targeted at the very idea that reasoning about conduct and values could prescribe policies. At best reason is the organisation of desires; all it can do is co-ordinate preferences and work out means to their satisfaction. David Hume drew this conclusion when in his *Treatise of*

Human Nature (1739) he wrote that 'reason is and can only be the slave of the passions'; and his 'instrumental' view has been adopted by most contemporary theories of individual and social choice which eschew any ambition to try to decide what we *should* desire or what we *should* want.

Notwithstanding these claims, however, it is significant that we still seek unifying and ennobling visions. We live in an age that is supposed to be post-ideological, yet all around one can see attempts to re-construct old narratives or to fashion new ones. No quarter passes without somebody producing a book on the modern mind, or the condition of society, and although these are often pessimistic they are also struggling to try and answer the questions of who we are, of what we have become, and of where we ought to be heading. The pressing issue, therefore, is whether such efforts are in vain.

Consider the situation in the area of creative culture. Postmodernist thinking has taken grip among art theorists raising the interesting question of where art, architecture, literature and music go 'after philosophy'. If one thinks of the history of European painting, for instance, it has long been an intellectually rich field, being informed at various stages by changing notions of the human person, the natural world and so on. It is not possible to study the work of artists like Giotto, Poussin or Claude Lorrain without seeing in their paintings certain interpretations of landscape as a bearer of significance, be it a different set of meanings in each case.

This is obviously true of religious art, but secular painting has also been resonant with moral and philosophical conceptions of human beings and their place in society and nature. People regularly ask such questions as whether we can still make inspiring art. The fear behind this is that somehow we have nothing 'meaningful' to say. Without an animating conception of humanity, portraiture is just a decorative form of documentation. If there is no idea imbuing the human image with meaning then all we have is a likeness, a mere resemblance. These worries are legitimate and

they have call forth at least three responses to the purported
loss of ideology.

The first involves going as in the past, but in a romantic
spirit, doubting that one can really ground practice in a
defensible philosophy. For example, one may continue with
the tradition of producing official portraits. Without philosophical conviction, however, this is apt to fail as serious
art. Contemporary portraits of western monarchs and pres-
idents are generally lacking in symbolic significance and
have little, if any, cultural resonance. There is neither awe
nor mystery; nor much sense of the artists recognising the
distinction between an office and the occupant of it. In the
past, official portraits were most often celebrating (or challenging) a role. The individuals were thought to be elevated
by the office, and official portraiture aimed to depict its
authority. Nowadays we find it near-to-impossible to think
in such terms. It is no surprise, therefore, that portraits of
heads of state are reduced to the status of pictures of afflu-
ent men and woman of a certain age. The response of the
romantic is to play with ideas of status and office, bringing
in various icons of these, but this is nostalgia-driven entertainment. The counterpart in building design is perhaps
more familiar: picking up features of Classical, Gothic and
other historical styles, but without really believing in any
philosophy of architecture.

The second response is one of self-conscious (and often
self-congratulatory) irony. Whereas romantic affirmation
involves entering into the spirit of an older order, even
though one cannot believe its ideological presuppositions,
the way of irony imposes no demands upon the intellect or
the imagination. It is simply a form of play. Without believing in its philosophical foundations, or even aspiring to
believe in them, one keeps quoting the forms of past culture.
This attitude is prominent in contemporary art and literature where authors deploy — with self-announcing irony —
the devices of certain genres. However, the practice of
cultural quotation is subject to diminishing returns. If one
simply draws from the stock of cultural forms without add-

ing to it, and is in turn drawn upon, a process of continuing impoverishment is established. Consider again the case of architecture and how in cities like Los Angeles the practice of making ironic reference to the styles of the eighteenth century has led very quickly to architects quoting recent postmodern buildings. Thereby the resources are diminished and the meaning of the original inspiration is lost.

The final response, and that which I favour, is one of reform and renewal. Standing firm in the face of postmodern criticism one questions whether the things that have been held to be problematic really are so, asking what precisely the problem is about transcendentalism, why universal humanism is untenable, and so on. And having been bold enough to challenge the various postmodern orthodoxies one may then consider the possibility of re-establishing confidence in some of the central philosophical and moral ideas of Western culture.

More precisely I believe we need a re-articulation of older conceptions of human nature, human values and public culture. In the first instance this may be a task for philosophers, but the various intellectual disciplines and the elements of deep culture such as the arts have an essential role to play if a sense of value and meaning is to become prevalent once more. Certainly one cannot operate as if 'modernity' had not been, and nor should one simply ignore the points made by postmodern critics. Reform and renewal are recurrent necessities in any living tradition: naive premodernism is not an option; and the idea of a Golden Age untroubled by scepticism is a fantasy of the ignorant. But before we try to finesse older ways of thinking we need first to show that they are not bankrupt.

There are, I think, two ways in which one might do this. One proceeds by example. If compelling instances can be produced of things having value, then nihilism is refuted. Any complete refutation of this sort would have to proceed area by area and value by value. That is not something I can do here; though in subsequent chapters several areas of value: intellectual, cultural, political, moral and aesthetic, will be discussed. Let me say something, however, if all too briefly, about the second way of proceeding. This is to show that our best understanding of human affairs is one in which questions of value and meaning arise both for individuals and for communities.

Some questions about values are psychological and sociological. Biographers and historians are interested in the ideals that motivated people; and periodically there are surveys of social attitudes designed to keep track of changes in the prevalent standards and principles of morality. These are empirical questions to be investigated and answered by sophisticated social science methods. But however successful these means may be, all they can tell us about are people's attitudes and behaviour. They cannot settle the many particular questions that people ask about what is good and bad, right and wrong; and nor can they settle the more abstract question of what it is for something to be good or bad, meaningful or meaningless. It is part of the human form of life to deliberate and act in accord with reasons—to find meaning. We have engaged in philosophy throughout the last two millennia and there is no serious reason to think that we will not continue to do so in the next one. Nihilism poses no threat—unless we adopt it.

Two

Making Sense of the Universe

The literary and intellectual traditions of Scotland, particularly in the modern period, are well known and much honoured in North America, not least because of the considerable influence of Scots (and Scots-Irish) thinkers on the development of political thought and educational practice there. Those thinkers were most often clergymen. The names of Francis Hutcheson (1694–1746), James Oswald (1703–93), Thomas Reid (1710–96), David Fordyce (1711–51), George Campbell (1719–96), Adam Ferguson (1723–1815), John Witherspoon (1723–94), and Alexander Gerard (1728–95), all Presbyterian ministers, come to mind; but they are only the most prominent in an imported Caledonian tradition that sought to combine rigorous philosophical thought and theologically-informed, Christian belief.

It is often supposed that this tradition began in the eighteenth century and lasted not long into the nineteenth. Yet the Ayrshire born, and Glasgow and Edinburgh educated, philosopher James McCosh (1811–94), took up post as the eleventh President of the College at Princeton in 1868, a full century to the year after Witherspoon's appointment; and in recalling his undergraduate studies at the University of Vermont (1875–79) John Dewey observed that 'Teachers of philosophy were at that time, almost to a man, clergymen' given to the 'Scotch Philosophy'.

While Aberdeen, Glasgow, St Andrews and other parts of the country played important roles in the emergence of the Scottish Enlightenment and in its cultural succession, Edinburgh was its pre-eminent site. In 1771, three years after the founding of the *Encyclopedia Britannica* there, Tobias Smollett coined the phrase 'hot bed of genius' to describe the city (in *The Expedition of Humphry Clinker*); and the minister and pamphleteer Dr Alexander Carlyle wrote of 'how fine a time it was when we could collect [for supper in an Edinburgh tavern] David Hume, Adam Smith, Adam Ferguson, Lord Elibank, and Drs. Blair and Jardine, on an hour's warning'.

Books and ideas remain central to the life of the city, as to that of its western cousin Glasgow and to the culture of Scotland more generally; and religion continues to have an influence, though its diminished role reflects the general weakening of the churches in Western Europe. Among the opening sessions of the 2005 Edinburgh International Book Festival, however, was a symposium on the famous Gifford Lectures, entitled *Science, Religion and Ethics*, followed by a conference at the University on *The Gifford Lectures: Retrospect and Prospect*.

The Gifford Lectures were established by the Scottish lawyer Lord Gifford, for the stated purposes of 'promoting, advancing, teaching and diffusing the study of "Natural Theology" in the widest sense of the term — in other words, "the Knowledge of God … the knowledge of His nature and attributes, [and] the knowledge of the relations which men and the whole universe bear to Him"'. In 1847 Adam Gifford attended a series of talks in Edinburgh by the American poet and philosopher Ralph Waldo Emerson — his presence there marking something of the developing desire of Americans to give back in kind to the Scots from whom they had acquired a taste for philosophical and religious ideas. These talks influenced Gifford's own thinking in the direction of metaphysics and transcendentalism, and they may have been an inspiration for his later decision to endow a lecture series in philosophy and religion.

The scale of his benefaction was enormous by the standards of the time: £80,000 — equivalent to about £6 million today. Even so, Gifford appears to have envisaged the lectures in local terms and probably did not imagine that they would become the principal forum for intellectual reflection on natural theology. The process of internationalization began early. In 1901 William James introduced his own lectures on *The Varieties of Religious Experience* by referring to 'a soil as sacred to the American imagination as that of Edinburgh'. He then added 'Let me say only that now that the current, here and at Aberdeen, has begun to run from west to east, I hope it may continue to do so. As years go by I hope that many of my countrymen may be asked to lecture in Scottish universities, changing places with Scotsmen lecturing in the States'.

The first Giffords began in 1889 with three series of lectures by, respectively, the Hegelean philosopher James Stirling, the philologist Friedrich Muller, and the Scots-born literary figure Andrew Lang. Subsequent lecturers have included historians, scientists and theologians, but philosophers have dominated overall. It may be instructive, therefore, to consider how their preoccupations have changed over the past one hundred and twenty years. Setting out a list of philosophers and the themes of their Gifford lectures from the first (Stirling's *Philosophy and Theology*) to the very recent (Simon Blackburn, 'Reason's Empire', published as *Truth: A Guide for the Perplexed*), and grouping the lectures into four roughly quarter-centuries proceeding from the end of the nineteenth to the start of the twenty-first, a number of features reveal themselves.

For the first three-quarters, all lecturers were male; but beginning with Hannah Arendt in 1972, lecturing on *The Life of the Mind*, a series of women have contributed, including some of the most notable philosophers of the period. Iris Murdoch (1981–82) lectured on *Metaphysics as a Guide to Morals*; Mary Hesse (1983–84) on 'The Construction of Reality'; Mary Midgley (1989–90) on *Science and Salvation*; Mary Warnock (1991–92) on *Imagination and Understanding*;

Martha Nussbaum (1993–94) on *Need and Recognition*, Onora O'Neill (2000–01) on *Autonomy and Trust in Bioethics*; Lynne Baker (2001–02) on *The Nature and Limits of Human Understanding*; and Eleonore Stump (2003–04) on *Wandering in the Darkness*.

The trend to include American women academics continued with the 2006 Edinburgh series delivered by the social theorist and theologian Jean Bethke Elshtain. Interestingly her title *Sovereign God, Sovereign State, Sovereign Self* echoes that of a work by Murdoch — *The Sovereignty of the Self*. It may be significant that the women lecturers have tended to explore issues that situate traditional philosophical questions within a context of broader meaning or value, but it might be unwise to make too much of that since it may be a trend within recent philosophy more generally. I will return to this later.

If one looks beyond the sex of the lecturers to the themes explored, a broader pattern would seem to be as follows. To begin with the lecturers adopted grand themes in which some vast issue was yoked to the idea of deity, or of the religious. Thus we have William James (1900–02) on *The Varieties of Religious Experience*; Pringle-Pattison (1911–13) on *The Idea of God in the Light of Recent Philosophy*; William Sorley (1913–15) *Moral Values and the Idea of God*; and Samuel Alexander (1916–18) *Space, Time and Deity*.

Next come strands of personal, cultural or historical self-reflection, some suggesting degrees of doubt or anxiety. Thus, A.E Taylor (1926–28) *The Faith of a Moralist*; John Dewey (1928–29) *The Quest for Certainty*; Etienne Gilson (1930–32) *The Spirit of Medieval Philosophy*; R.B. Perry (1946–48) *A Critique of Civilisation*; Gabriel Marcel (1948–50) *The Mystery of Being*; John Wisdom (1948–50) *The Mystery of the Transcendental*; and H.J. Paton (1949–50) *The Modern Predicament*. No doubt the effects and anticipations of world wars were influences here, but something more narrowly philosophical, namely skepticism, can also be detected.

In the next quarter (1950–75) the self-reflection that had earlier thinkers linking the objects of their speculation to their own interests then seemed to push thinkers back into preoccupation with thought and action and with the thinking-acting subject itself. In this vein we have Brand Blanshard (1951–53) *Reason*; Michael Polanyi (1951–52) *Personal Knowledge*; John MacMurray (1952–54) *The Self as Agent* and *Persons in Relation*; C.A. Campbell (1953–55) *On Selfhood and Godhood*. Georg von Wright (1958–60) *The Varieties of Goodness*. H.B. Price (1959–61) *Belief*; and H.D. Lewis (1966–68) *The Elusive Mind* and *The Elusive Self*.

By the middle 70s, and on to the present, the gaze seems to have returned outward: sometimes 'vertically' to the transcendent, though often 'horizontally' to the community. Thus we find Stephen Clark (1981–82) *The Love of Wisdom and the Love of God*; Richard Swinburne (1982–84) *The Evolution of the Soul*; Antony Flew (1986–87) *The Logic of Mortality*; Alvin Plantinga (1987–88) on *Our Knowledge of God* and then in 2005 on *Science and Religion*; Alasdair MacIntyre (1987–88) *Three Rival Versions of Moral Enquiry*; Hilary Putnam (1990–91) on *Renewing Philosophy*; Michael Dummett (1996–97) on *Thought and Reality*; Holmes Rolston III (1997–98) *Genes, Genesis and God*; Charles Taylor (1998–99) on *Living in a Secular Age*; Ralph McInerny (1999–2000) on *The Preambles of Faith*; Peter van Inwagen (2003–04) *The Problem of Evil*; and myself, John Haldane (2005) on *Mind, Soul and Deity*.

I have omitted from the last half-century, historical series examining the ideas of past figures and periods. The history of philosophy has grown in significance, particularly in the last quarter of the twentieth century, in part for reasons of professional crowding: for with more people entering academic life, turning from x to the history of x doubles the opportunities for scholarship. There is, however, a deeper reason, I believe, for the growth of historical studies and this connects with features of the recent period which I would like to comment upon.

When Lord Gifford conceived the idea of a lectureship 'to promote and diffuse the study of Natural Theology' the professional and educated middle classes in Britain were still generally religious and overwhelmingly Christian.

Certainly there had been challenges to Bible and Creed from natural science, philosophy and the historical method of biblical scholarship; but atheism remained a dangerous eccentricity and avowed agnosticism was still rare. Among the intellectuals, however, things were different. While it was not yet supposed that 'the content of a statement could not extend beyond the possibility of its empirical verification' nonetheless it was widely presumed that what could not be brought before actual or possible perception was at least problematic if not impossible. At the same time, the idea that scripture might be treated as historical testimony amounting to evidence was felt to be naïve; and advances in natural science provided alternative hypotheses about the origins of human beings and of the material world more generally.

Religiously inclined philosophers presented two broad reactions to these developments. The first maintained the paradigm of knowledge as *observation*, and treated biblical narrative and religious discourse as forms of moral or spiritual commitment or aspiration; not reducing everything to science but leaving a space for feeling and acting in ways that while they could not be rationally justified nevertheless seemed to have value. The second reaction challenged empiricism itself, arguing for the holist view that everything is related to everything else, rather in the manner of rationally linked ideas. This 'idealist' alternative was certainly a contrast to empiricism, but so far as the content of traditional religion was concerned it tended once again to interpret it mythically or symbolically.

Idealism itself was attacked by Bertrand Russell and G.E. Moore at Cambridge (England), but then by others in North America, and a new realist temper began to develop. So far as religion was concerned it tended to be indifferent, when not either sceptical or actively hostile. Natural theology was marginalized as intellectual believers tended to avoid confrontation with mainstream philosophy and retreated instead to what I earlier termed personal, cultural or historical self-reflection.

In the second half of the twentieth century things began to change, and in a direction that Lord Gifford had hoped for, but the development came in stages. First, philosophers reconsidered their pictures of the thinking, acting subject. Various ideas about mind, action, and value, common in modern thought from the time of Descartes and Locke were judged to be problematic; and it was not unreasonable to suppose that their revision might produce ways of thinking more congenial to religious thought.

As it turned out, however, the rethinking of old philo-sophical ideas has led not so much to a new philosophy as to diversification of the practice into different schools, meth-ods, areas and applications. When Lord Gifford conceived the lectureship there was general agreement on the nature and value of academic philosophy but that has changed. For some academics and their followers, philosophy is a form of cultural critique principally directed towards subverting claims to knowledge. For others, it is a handmaid of natural science. For some, it is the place where claims for science as providing theories of everything can best be resisted. For others, philosophy is a form of ethical reflection, tending at one end to disinterested clarification, and at the other to pol-icy making. For others still, it is an exercise of the literary imagination, even a kind of poetry.

It is this diversity that accounts for the range of themes and approaches pursued in recent Gifford series. In the ear-lier part of the last quarter the diversity did not especially favour religious interests but that may be changing due to the development, in a world of specialism, of philosophy of religion as an expert-led field of enquiry. This could result in a concentration of future series around themes and approaches favoured by the leading practitioners of this specialism, converging with the growing interest among reflective scientists in the possibility that biology and cos-mology exhibit evidences of design.

It would be unfortunate, however, if the question of the place of religion in the larger scheme of things were left as a subject just for sociologists or historians. Perplexing as it may be to advocates of secularization, and notwithstanding predictions of the collapse of church membership in the West, the world is not becoming any less religious. Indeed there are signs of a growth of religious interest among the educated younger generations. The question, therefore, is not whether interested people will keep up with philosophers as they pursue their professional interests, but whether philosophers will stay close to thinking and enquiring folk.

If they hope to do so then they might profitably consider religious ideas about the nature, meaning and conduct of human life as much as issues in speculative philosophy of religion and metaphysics. In his recently published book *Truth: A Guide for the Perplexed*, deriving from his 2004 series, the Cambridge philosopher Simon Blackburn reveals a marked hostility to religion. Acknowledging Lord Gifford's religious commitment he begs to differ remarking that 'I do not believe that the gods of human beings do much credit to their inventors and interpreters'. A different attitude might have resulted had Blackburn reflected on the (unacknowledged) source of his subtitle. For, 'A Guide for the Perplexed' was originally the translated title of a work, *Moreh Nebuchim*, by the great twelfth century Jewish philosopher Moses Maimonides (Rabbi Moshe ben Maimon) concerning the reconciliation of philosophy and religion. That profound aspiration is also very much in keeping with the Scottish intellectual and cultural tradition that so impressed itself upon the American founders, and which continues to animate much American thought and practice today.

Three

Plain Talk and Common Sense Philosophy

In July of 2001 the University of Glasgow awarded Billy Connolly the honorary degree of Doctor of Letters. About thirty years before, he scandalised some and entertained others in the city with his adaptations of biblical narratives: providing a Glaswegian translation of the story of Moses, beginning 'Nip hame and get yer peepil ...' and offering a sketch about The Last Supper taking place in Glasgow's Gallowgate, not in Galilee, and being held in the Saracen's Head Inn ('Sarrie Heid') '... near the [Glasgow] Cross'.

The voice of Billy Connolly is immediately recognisable and, once heard, unforgettable. Even as he begins a story, hearers prepare to laugh at one of his memorable tales rendered in the currency of Glaswegian language and life. Indeed, for many his is the voice of Glasgow; and for some, perhaps, even the voice of Scotland. If the first fact is not universally welcomed within Glasgow itself (honorary degree notwithstanding); the second possibility is likely to cause distress to many Scots who would want to think of their land and people in more elevated, cultured and refined terms.

The actress Maggie Smith tells of how when she was preparing for the part of Miss Jean Brodie, and was having difficulty mastering the precise prim tone of the character, she was advised to spend the afternoon with some genteel woman from Edinburgh's 'Morningside' district. Phoning such a lady to invite her to afternoon tea, Maggie Smith complimented her on the fact that her accent was a perfect model for the Scottish type she wanted to perfect: '*Accent!*' ('*exent*') exclaimed the lady — 'I most certainly do not have an *accent!*'

The vocal contrast between this good lady and Dr Connolly is obvious enough; but behind and beneath it lie vast volumes of cultural difference. You could mark these by a series of textured oppositions: rough and smooth, coarse and refined, granular and creamy, pitted and polished; but these are all fairly gross generalisations and fail in any case to go very deep. Approached from another direction you might say that while Glasgow is unashamedly Scottish, and only nominally British; Edinburgh exhibits an Anglicising tendency to the extent — at the extreme — of hoping not to attract attention to itself as conspicuously lying over the border.

This distinction is connected with diverse attitudes to physical labour and material production. Although Glasgow in the West and Edinburgh in the East are separated by only forty miles, their efforts and achievements are markedly different. The first is home to two of the most famous football teams of all time, Celtic and Rangers; the second is host to the largest arts festival in Europe. The one was for long a place of manufacture and trade; the other a centre of law, medicine and administration. Each city is set close by water's edge, and each grew in consequence of foreign trade. But whereas Edinburgh's wealth came early on, and established it as the Royal Capital of Scotland from the fifteenth century; the period of Glasgow's affluence and growth began in the late eighteenth century, and continued up to the first World War.

The sea passage from Glasgow to America was the shortest by far from any British port across the Atlantic. As the colonies in Virginia and Maryland grew, so did the transatlantic trade; bringing tobacco and cotton eastwards, and carrying manufactured goods, including finished cloth, West to the Americas. Scotland's first millionaires came from the group of Glasgow's tobacco lords. Cotton and textile industries were later joined by ironworks and shipbuilding. In 1802 the steamship *Charlotte Dundas* was launched on the Forth and Clyde Canal, and within thirty years another hundred steam vessels had been built, mostly on the Clyde. For more than a century following, shipbuilding was a main source of employment, and it was in a Clydeside shipyard in the Govan area that Billy Connolly first went to work.

Two centuries earlier, in 1762, one Revd Thom, the Church of Scotland Minister of Govan, wrote to the University of Glasgow to complain about the uselessness, for what he described as 'an industrious and commercial people', of the classical education which the University was proud to provide. That early pragmatist demand for a useful and vocational training, came at a time when in Edinburgh clerics were worrying about the corrosive effects of intellectual speculation upon religious faith. People are generally familiar with the distress caused among the Victorians by Darwin's theory of man's natural descent; but less well-known are the eighteenth century speculation of Lord Monboddo who was made a Scottish judge around the time of Revd Thom's letter; and who advanced the view that men were related to monkeys.

Monboddo was one of a group of intellectuals who formed the Scottish Enlightenment, and whose other members included the philosopher David Hume and the philosopher and economist Adam Smith. It would be wrong to suggest that these gentlemen had little interest in practical matters of commerce and economy. In fact Hume was at one point a counting-clerk in Bristol, and later turned to diplomacy and administration, being secretary to the ambassador in Paris, and under-secretary of state in London for what was then known as 'the northern Department' the precursor to the Scottish Office. Smith, of course, was author of the founding text of economics, *The Wealth of Nations* (1776), and he ended his life as Commissioner of customs in Edinburgh.

Their primary interests, however, were speculative and theoretical; and the drift of their thought carried them away from the dour, gritty Calvinism of the Kirk, into a realm of humanistic enlightenment: a bright world of detached reflection on the workings of the human mind. Seventeen years before publishing the *Wealth of Nations*, Smith produced his great work of moral philosophy, the *Theory of Moral Sentiments* (1759). In this he followed his friend Hume in arguing that judgements of right and wrong, good and bad, virtue and vice, are not founded on reason, or rooted in religious revelation, but are expressions of human emotion — as Hume had put it in the *Treatise*: 'sentiments of approbation and of disapprobation arising within the human breast' as men contemplate actions of one kind or another.

Just as for Hume morality lies in the human mind, not in a world of moral facts; so our beliefs about the world itself are human conjectures fashioned on the basis of impressions of colour, shape, sound, odour, taste and texture. Hume's account of knowledge as based in experience is in the tradition of British empiricism, but Hume was much more radical than had been John Locke in the previous century.

Generations of philosophers going all the way back to Aristotle had emphasised the importance of sense-experience as a source of knowledge; and the scholastics of the middle ages had even formulated the slogan 'there is nothing in the intellect that was not just in the senses'; but until the seventeenth and eighteenth century philosophers assumed that what was 'in the senses' was experience of the world itself. The open eye looks upon the world; the ear attends to the tread of the foot, the rustle of the leaves, the tinkle of the glass.

What Hume from his Edinburgh study insisted upon, however, was that all that we can *really* claim to know are mental impressions themselves. The blurriness of the world as seen by the short-sighted, or the intoxicated, is not a perception of a blurred world; but the experience of images *within* the viewer himself. More generally, the proper objects of experience are features of, and in, the mind. Hume allowed that from them we naturally infer the existence and condition of an outer world of objects related in various ways. We naturally form beliefs about the existence of others, about the furniture of the world, and about the various relations and processes that cement it all together. But these are all *conjectures*, constructed out of internal impressions and the mind's own tendency to project order and regularity outwards. And then, this done, it appears to discover them as external facts, from which all sorts of scientific and even theological conclusions might be derived. If Hume were right, however, this whole edifice of seemingly objective knowledge would have been shown to be no more substantial than a dream.

Immanuel Kant wrote of how reading Hume's sceptical philosophy awoke him from his own 'dogmatic slumber' where hitherto he had taken the world for granted; now he saw that it had to be proved to exist. Whether Kant was ever successful in producing such a proof is a matter of some debate; but I want now to bring on to the scene Hume's greatest domestic critic, and perhaps his greatest and most effective critic ever, namely his contemporary Thomas Reid.

Reid was born in the Aberdeenshire manse of his father. For generations since the Reformation the family had numbered ministers of the Church of Scotland, and that was also to be Reid's own vocation. Like Kant, however, he took flight as a philosopher upon being startled by the implications of Hume's philosophy.

Reid had two arguments against Hume: first that the implications of his philosophy were so extensive, so radical, and so disruptive of scientific, moral and religious thought, as well as of common sense, that any principle or premise from which they derived must itself be suspect. His second argument was that Hume's starting point is itself wholly unwarranted. Where Hume claims that what we are acquainted with are visual and other sensory impressions, Reid insists that what we know are how things themselves look. Seen through weak eyes things appear blurry, heard through failing ears, sounds seem muffled; but if we are to make any sense of this, then it must be on the basis of distinguishing between things themselves, and the ways in which they are experienced. And in doing this we see that far from the world being constructed out of the mind; it is the *mind* that is informed and filled from without, as we come into contact with the *world*.

This philosophy of 'common-sense' was first fashioned in Reid's native Aberdeenshire, but in 1763 he was appointed to the Professorship of Moral Philosophy at the University of Glasgow in succession to Adam Smith, and it was from there that he published his responses to Hume's sceptical philosophy, beginning in 1764 with his *Enquiry into the human Mind on the Principles of Common Sense*, and continuing for another 30 years until his death age 86. A few years ago I had occasion to edit Reid's last piece of philosophical writing, an essay on the subjects of agency and causality entitled 'Of Power', and was much impressed by the strength of his hand and the clarity of his prose.

It was also from Glasgow that Reid's philosophy was carried across the Atlantic to the Americas where it had enormous influence right up to the twentieth century. The pragmatist philosopher John Dewey, sometimes described as 'America's last public intellectual', and who died in 1952, recounts how as an undergraduate he was educated on the philosophical principles of Scottish clergymen. Those principles were versions, sometimes confused, of Reid's philosophy of common sense.

Besides the stark opposition in their philosophies, there was also a marked contrast in the character of Hume and of Reid, something of which emerges in two contemporary portraits. We know from correspondence and contemporary accounts that both were gentle and amiable spirits, but the portraits show a difference that marks the two Scotlands of the period. Alan Ramsay's portrait of Hume (in the Scottish National Portrait Gallery in Edinburgh) shows a somewhat soft faced, sensual lipped, fleshy figure, dressed in brocaded scarlet coat with lace cuffs and cravat. It serves to confirm Hume's account of his life and style while living in Paris: of which he wrote: 'Here I feed on ambrosia, drink nothing but nectar, breathe incense only, and walk on flowers'.

Sir Henry Raeburn's portrait of Reid (now at Fyvie Castle, Aberdeenshire) shows a very different figure. Where Hume is seen full face looking contentedly at the viewer; Reid is set at three-quarters and looks seriously if not severely, into empty space: his mind directed upon some religious piety or philosophical rectitude. The lips are thin, the nose long, the bony contour evident. Like his philosophy, Reid's life stayed close to the realities of the world as he encountered them in an increasingly mercantile and industrial Glasgow.

In 1773 he was visited there by Boswell and Johnson on their way back from the tour of the Western Highlands. At that time mail coaches arriving at the Gallow Gate in the east of the city would be met by waiters dressed in embroidered coats, red breeches and powdered hair sent from the Saracen's Head Inn. Here it was, two centuries before Billy Connolly imagined the last supper being held there, that the weary travellers entertained the distinguished and well known professor, along with two of his colleagues from the university of which Connolly is now an honorary graduate.

Boswell notes that the hospitality ran to both breakfast and supper, but of the day's conversation he records nothing beyond remarking that 'the professors ... did not venture to expose themselves much to the battery of cannon which they knew might play upon them'. Reid may have judged that this was not the occasion for philosophical discourse; or perhaps he engaged in it but it passed Boswell by. Certainly Dr Johnson did not find it easy to absorb philosophical opinions that seemed to strain his sense of the ordinary. Famously he once sought to demolish a philosophical theory related to Hume's (that of Bishop Berkeley) by kicking a stone and announcing 'I refute it thus!'. Perhaps he also had difficulty with Reid's view, for although Reid's philosophy may have been technically commonsensical, being philosophy it may yet not have been all that obvious. It would be interesting to hear Billy Connolly using his plain talk to communicate this sort of common sense. Were he to do so, the setting of the Saracen's Head would be doubly ironic in just the sort of way that should appeal to a Doctor of Letters.

Four

Making Sense of Society

Politics shades into political philosophy. Pursue questions about any social policy issue far enough, and a principle or a basic orientation comes into view. Such orientations tend towards one of three political values: *social well-being* (including the common interest, or as it is increasingly termed the 'common good'); *contractual justice* (often expressed in terms of civil rights and responsibilities); and *personal liberty* (the freedom of the individual). While these are not exhaustive possibilities, nor wholly mutually exclusive of one another, they are—like magnetic poles— constant points of guidance, and distinct sources of attraction and repulsion.

In the 1950s and 60s, politicians of the left were transfixed by the ideal of promoting the collective good, and they directed economic and social policy to this end. Some insisted on nothing less than complete 'social possession' of the means of production, exchange and control. Others were content to restrict state ownership to basic industries. At the same time, education, housing, welfare, transport, and other fundamentals of modern life came under exten- sive state control as part of the effort to deploy 'national resources' in the common interest. In the 1970s collectivism gave way, among social democrats, to a more nuanced concern with justice, as the recognition grew that citizens are participants in, and not just patients of the state.

In his classic work of political philosophy *A Theory of Justice* (1971) John Rawls expressed this understanding through a reworking of the old idea of the social contract. The fundamental requirement on the state is that it treats all citizens fairly or justly. For a society to be fair, however, its basic political arrangements must be such as would be agreed to by any rational person who might find themselves a member of that society, but who did not know in advance what his or her social and economic position within it might be. Thus, you or I might tolerate economic and social inequalities related to ability and achievement, but only if provision is made for the disadvantaged. After all, we might be fortunate, but equally we might not be.

This recognition of the need for citizens to be willing participants, in turn opened the door to the political right in Britain and America who placed great emphasis on the priority of the individual over the contract. Ironically, in the United States it was a close Harvard colleague of Rawls (and one whom he greatly admired) namely Robert Nozick, who writing in *Anarchy State and Utopia* (1974) diminished to vanishing point the claims of society and argued that progressive taxation was an attack upon the right of the individual to hold and to transfer property. Freely giving one's money to others is one thing, having it taken away and distributed by a third party is another. On this account non-voluntary taxation for welfare, for example, is not an expression of justice but a form of state theft. In later years Nozick moderated his position, but the influence of his and others' 'libertarian' ideas has been profound.

Nearly three decades on from the intellectual defeat of socialism where do we stand now? Thatcher and Reagan seemed to represent the conclusion of a post-war ideological debate which had moved from the collective *good*, via contractual *justice* to individual *liberty*. Since then, however, a new kind of consensus politics appeared to be with us. Occasionally characterised as 'pragmatism', it looked to be represented in a reticent form by John Major's Conservative vision of a nation 'at ease with itself', and in an assertive one by Tony Blair's 'New Labour: New Britain'. As seemed clear at the time, and as has become ever more apparent since, the issues at recent elections were not so much ideological as managerial. New Labour promised to deliver a less fractious, less corrupt and more effective form of government, but it left unchallenged the Thatcherite legacy in economics and in privatisation. Indeed, it was careful to suggest that this might well be protected and even enhanced — hence the wish of Tony Blair and even of Gordon Brown to associate themselves with aspects of the Thatcherite economic revolution. Recall that one of Brown's first acts as Chancellor was to give control of interest rates to the Bank of England. In practice as in theory, Labour no longer seeks the means of production, exchange and control. The ideological battles of the twentieth century are over.

But perhaps not. Certainly there is absolutely no suggestion of a return to socialism. Tony Blair and his principal associates evidently have distaste even for the very term, let alone for those for whom it is a regimental badge worn with pride. This fact was not lost on many of the New Labour MPs who hoped for advancement and were wary of saying and doing anything that might suggest 'unsoundness' (to use a rather Tory expression). I sometimes wonder whether anyone in Number Ten or Millbank Tower found themselves slipping into the Thatcherite habit of describing a left-leaning dissident as 'not one of us', or as a 'wet'. Perhaps such words would be voiced in an ironic tone, but I doubt that they would be any less sincerely meant.

At the same time as distancing itself from socialism, however, New Labour retained moral aspirations for society. Following the 1997 election I published an article in *The Times* in which I suggested that a process might be underway designed to effect significant changes in the values of British society. I linked this to the unprecedented grouping of Scots in senior government posts, noting that there is a long tradition north of the border of serious moral thinking: from Celtic missionaries to Protestant reformers and from Adam Smith and David Hume to present day church leaders and social commentators. Some wag—not me—gave these reflections the title 'The Celtic Conversion of England'. I had suggested, only a little less evangelically, 'A Scottish Mission to England' (part of this article appears incorporated within the next chapter 'A Disuniting Kingdom?').

Whatever its title, and notwithstanding its apparently welcoming tone, the article carried a barb which I was relieved to discover some readers had noted. For while commending Mr Blair's concern with social morality, I suggested that it is not enough to sing the songs of virtue while seeking to avoid a major ethical question such as abortion which bristles with moral, political and legal difficulties. To this I might now add euthanasia, reproductive technology, and traditional family structure. Likewise, I suggested that the promotion of a politics rooted in specifically Judaeo-Christian virtues was likely to meet with opposition from advocates of moral individualism. To quote:

> There are reasons for doubting whether New Labour's term of office will see improvements in the moral condition of government and of society. Many of its supporters in the urban middle class, particularly in London, are detached from traditional communities, and celebrate their rejection of conformity to older social norms. These supporters also give emphasis to freedom of choice as against habits of acceptance, self-sacrifice and duty.

The implied challenge to stand fast to what was being proclaimed was accompanied by the thought that the task of moral reconstruction might begin where the soil of community lies deepest, in Scotland, and in the north of England.

In an interesting and timely article published in *The Times* a few days later, one of its regular commentators, Matthew Parris, also took the measure of New Labour and found it no less possessed of habits of orthodoxy and authoritarianism than its recently deceased parent—the Labour Party of Foot and Kinnock. He also found it given to what he regarded as a disturbing form of moral evangelism. Generously, he complimented my suggestion that the new Government has a Celtic spirit of reform that puts it at odds with rootless self-indulgent individualists. However, he then continued

as an Englishman, I find it odious. I shudder at the phrase
[Haldane] celebrates: 'Moral community'. Not everyone
will thank 'the missionaries of St Columba' whom he com-
mends, for sending south this type of priggish, sourly self-
satisfied, net-curtain twitching, neighbourhood police
mentality.

Though wittily expressed, this was an uncharacteristically
shrill reaction. Higher and better questions are at issue.
Matthew Parris regards a spirit intolerant of self-indulgent
individualism as 'odious' and shudders at the idea of
'moral community'. Of course, glossed in a certain way a
concern for the moral condition of society can be made to
seem threatening. But it is precisely the libertarian,
moral-privatisation tendency within the Conservative
party, of which he was a Parliamentary member from 1979
to 1986, having previously worked in the Party's Research
Department and then served as Mrs Thatcher's correspondence secretary, that detached it from the Tory tradition of
balancing individual freedom and the common good. Perhaps Parris would counter with the claim that the value of
liberty must never be compromised or lost sight of. The
most noble and effective liberalism, however, is a sensibility
tolerant of difference, not one indifferent to moral values.
Each leader of the modern Conservatives has had to find a
point at which he or she could achieve equilibrium in a
developed posture that combined a tilt towards liberty and
another towards conformity. David Cameron has yet to
recognise the inevitability of attempting this balancing feat
and is still wandering the stage in search of an act — and an
audience.

The public and the private, and the moral and the political, are convenient classifications, but in reality they do not
mark out wholly separate spheres. I very much doubt that
Matthew Parris and those who would express themselves
in similar terms *really* believe that it is no business of political society to advance or protect any particular idea of the
human good; any more than bishops who say that the
Church welcomes everyone whatever their lifestyles *really*
believe that unrepentant evil is 'OK by Jesus'. Ought society

and the Churches not to take a line on child abuse and racism, and instead regard each as legitimate lifestyle options? We all engage in rhetoric to advance our claims; the wise are those who know when they are doing this, and who also know when to stop.

At any rate, the truth of the matter, once especially well understood by Conservatives and Christian Socialists, is that morality does and should shape the public sphere. If the libertarian fantasy of a disinterested state is set aside the question then becomes one of how the values of liberty and of community are to be worked together. That is not easy to answer, nor is the answer the same for all times and for all places. We have yet to see how well New Labour and 'New'(?) Tory address the issue. As regards the first, the initial efforts at an ethical foreign policy were impaired by evident uncertainty as to just what this might involve, and by the disaster of the Iraq war. Meanwhile, on the domestic front, successive Home Secretaries' appetites for strong measures seems less a matter of political philosophy and more one of personality, or opportunism. So far as the Tories are concerned, three leaders on from the defeat of 1997, it may yet be some while before they are sufficiently settled to deal with these matters.

In addition, there is the question of how well the Scots can manage to display virtue in the conduct of their own national affairs. The devolved Parliament offers the opportunity for this and I hope it will be taken. Yet it is hard to resist the thought that its business will continue to be conducted in the manner of a borough council. For reasons which I do not understand, non-Anglicised Scottish politicians often seem to be either cultured, genteel, and largely unsuited to government — save perhaps as benevolent viceroys (Donald Dewar and Menzies Campbell come to mind) — or else chancers who look to be on the make .

However, having mentioned that the Parliament may offer the opportunity for morally-informed policy making, let me provide a couple of suggestions for early consideration by it. Social and scientific developments have added new ethical problems to the stock of old ones. While individual responsibility remains primary there is a role for political society in providing education and guidance, particularly in relation to medicine and emerging technologies. Additionally, through the state, society must set limits to methods of research, and to its clinical applications. More generally there is a need for a national ethics committee (of the sort which successive Westminster administrations have refused to establish), charged with the task of producing consultations on major ethical questions, and of maintaining a directory of ethics committees within the professions and public institutions; and empowered to put recommendations to the national Parliament for deliberation and action. If this poses a challenge to the Labour government's decision as what powers are reserved to Westminster and Whitehall then so be it. Such a clash will come sooner or later and I would prefer to think that the subject might be a noble one.

Returning to the philosophical foundations of politics allow me to echo the literary style of the Scottish enlightenment and say that the fellowship of society is natural and necessary for mankind and that it is better that men and women act out of shared values and common interests than under the direction of law. Thus while there is a case for restrictive legislation in some areas, the Scottish Parliament should aim to promote the development of civil society — that large and indefinite cluster of groupings that lies above the individual and the family but below the level of the state. Pursuit of this aim would mean that wherever possible responsibilities should be transferred away from the state to churches, community organisations, professional groupings, schools, colleges and universities, etc.

Such policies should have great appeal to those who recognise the need to balance the interests of the individual and the needs of the group, and who see in this balance the possibility of reconciling the values with which I began, those of liberty, justice and the common good. Policies designed to respect and to promote the family and civil associations have the potential to strengthen society and to establish a barrier to the tyranny of the state. Were they to be adopted and effectively implemented north of the Tweed it might not be long before they were exported — south of the border down Westminster way. Before then, however, Scottish politics and the culture of ideas have to be got into shape and brought together. There is much work to be done.

Five

A Disuniting Kingdom?

In 1997 Scotland celebrated the 1400th anniversary of the death of St Columba (known in Gaelic as *'Colmcille'* — Colm of the Churches). His journey from Ireland to Iona in 563 initiated the spread of Celtic Christianity throughout Western Europe. It was a missionary movement associated with reform, self-discipline and a recall to virtue. In due course, it gave way to the more urbane monasticism of St Benedict, but the fact remains that the Celtic influence on Europe was of immense cultural and moral importance. It has often been said that the Celtic Christianity saved Europe from barbarism.

In July of that anniversary year the *New York Times* published an editorial piece by Karl Meyer. Entitled 'The Genius of Scotland' it argued that it is good news for Britain, and 'for all of us', that Scotland and those it has borne are having a significant impact on science and society. His two examples were the cloning of a sheep by the Roslyn geneticists and the election to government of Tony Blair's New Labour Party. Meyer went on to relate these events to the long tradition of benign innovation associated with Scotland, and he attributed this national virtue to the country's education system. As he observed 'In the 18th century ... Scottish schools were generations ahead of those elsewhere ... Well into the 19th century the Scots supported four universities to England's two ... in Georgian times Scotland

33

graduated 10,000 doctors to England's 500, and one in four British regimental officers was Scottish'.

Whatever one's view of Tony Blair and Dolly the sheep, it is undeniable that given its size and relative lack of wealth Scotland has been remarkably productive of men (and women) of ideas — *and of action*. From Celtic Christianity to the Protestant Reformation, and from Adam Smith and David Hume to Lord Reith and Cardinal Winning, Scottish life has been marked by a degree of concern for social morality that has generally been lacking south of the border. This fact may be of more than merely historical and sociological interest. It may be Britain's hope.

Remarkably, at the time of Meyer's editorial the Prime Minister, the Chancellor of the Exchequer, the Foreign Secretary, the Chief Secretary to the Treasury, the Economic Secretary, the Secretary of State for Defence, the Minister for Europe, the Lord Chancellor, and the Solicitor General, were *all* Scots, to one degree or another. Given this unprecedented national grouping in government, and Scots moral evangelism, it would have been surprising if there were not ambitions to effect deep changes in British society.

In the 1980s a criticism of Western liberal societies began to be voiced. This held that they are overly-individualistic and committed to moral neutrality in public life. Consequently, they are unable to recognise, let alone to promote the virtues of moral communities. This 'communitarian challenge' has become something of an orthodoxy among political theorists and the politicians they have influenced. One of its authors is the Scots-Irish philosopher Alasdair MacIntyre who is much quoted in social democratic circles. MacIntyre, who is a convert to Roman Catholicism, is also favoured by religiously-inclined public figures.

In his book *The Politics of Hope*, deriving from lectures first given in St Andrews, Chief Rabbi Jonathan Sacks quotes MacIntyre with approval. Subsequently, MacIntyre reviewed the book in the Catholic weekly *The Tablet*. Though generally favourable, he noted two points of difficulty facing the programme of family and community renewal that Sacks would like to see implemented in Britain. First, the effects of markets upon conditions of work; and second the cynicism of modern governments which are forever preoccupied with securing the support of heterogeneous and competing social groups.

The problem is that modern societies are de-moralised and culturally fragmented. All that remain as bases for policy-making are appeals to personal advantage, or to threat of alien domination. Interestingly, these negative themes featured prominently in the Tories 1997 election campaign: vote Labour and watch taxes rise and British interests be sold out to Europe. New Labour, by contrast, made much of rectitude in public life, economic justice at home, and a blend of morality and pragmatism in foreign policy.

Aside from cynicism about the seriousness of a new administration's adherence to virtue, there were two reasons for doubting whether New Labour's term of office would see improvements in the moral condition of government and of society. First, there is the issue of social fragmentation; and second there is that of liberal neutrality or progressivism in matters of personal morality. Many of the urban middle-class who support New Labour, particularly in London, are detached from traditional communities, and celebrate their rejection of conformity to older social norms. These supporters also give emphasis to freedom of choice as against habits of acceptance, self-sacrifice and duty. Witness in this regard the marginalisation of *Labour for Life* and Tony Blair's personal discomfort over the abortion issue.

Consider, however, the following. The difficulties mentioned are most acute in London and other large southern cities. As one moves north, the soil of moral community grows deeper. Cross the border and one enters another country with its own religious tradition, and its own education and legal systems. Until recently moral philosophy was more or less compulsory in Scottish universities and it is still pursued by large numbers of first year arts students. The Scottish population is better educated, more settled and more morally conservative than its English counterpart.

The class system is less pronounced and attitudes to Europe and the rest of the world are less xenophobic.

Out of this world grew the leading figures of the first New Labour cabinet and in particular a Prime Minister with a clear ambition to nurture a sense of moral community. That ambition was always fragile and liable to resistance from rootless, self-indulgent individualists and from pressure groups promoting interests rather than values. A better inner-government strategy is suggested by the lives and missions of Columba and his Celtic followers. They had first to establish strong moral communities within Scotland before they could venture further. One enduring benefit of their efforts, however, is a sense of the importance of morality and society, a sense transformed but not at all reduced by the Scottish Reformation and Enlightenment.

In short, the Blairite mission might have done well to establish itself first in Scotland and then move south through the old communities of Sunderland, Lancashire and Yorkshire building on the folk-memory of shared existence. By stages southern resistance to reform might have reduced or been less formidable. A Celtic 'reconversion' remains a possibility and the Tories may yet look back on the 1997 election defeat and realise that their greatest loss was Scotland. Amid all the ensuing discussion of the Tory leadership and the future of the party, little was said of the loss of Scottish one-nation Tories such as Malcolm Rifkind and Ian Lang, successive Secretaries of State for Scotland. That may have been a sign that the Conservatives had lost interest in the United Kingdom and retreated into a southern homeland. In neglecting Scotland, however, they aided the cause of Scottish nationalism, as ironically, in his failure to respect the traditional values of community, so too did Tony Blair.

The British Isles has long been admired as a model of political stability: home to the mother of Parliaments, ruled over by a constitutional monarch, and with ministerial accountability to the national assembly. For all that, however, the United Kingdom may be in its final stages, and if so its life as a unified state will have been a relatively short one. The 1800 Act of Union conjoined Ireland with Great Britain, which itself was the product of the union of the Scottish and English parliaments effected less than a century before in 1707. In both cases there had been prior forms of sovereign union between these kingdoms: with Henry VIII being declared King of Ireland in 1541, and James VI of Scotland ascending to the thrones of England and Ireland in 1603, thereby acquiring the further title of James I.

In the nineteenth century, Westminster governments spoke of the threat to the Union posed by the Irish question, and for the past four decades Republicans and Nationalists have done their best to end British rule on the island of Ireland. As in the past, however, the main key to the future of the UK lies with the Scots. Once again, as in 1706 there are parliaments north and south of the border, and as in 1603 a Scot has ascended to the leadership of the whole of Britain.

(Dr) Gordon Brown studied history at Edinburgh University and must have thought through the issues from every direction. In recent years he has been stressing the importance of British identity, most emphatically his own. Yet as Frank Field observed following one of Brown's declarations of the importance of the Union 'Every time he embraces Britishness it just emphasises his Scottishness. We know from the polls that the demand for independence is now stronger in England than it is in Scotland. So he should do the only sensible thing — embrace the English question'.

The present situation arises from the creation in 1999 of a devolved Scottish parliament. This was New Labour's response to the pressure within Scotland for a degree of home rule. As late as 1955 the Scottish Tory Unionists held a majority of the country's Westminster constituencies, but they came to be seen as representing the interests of an Anglicised aristocracy. Then the Thatcher revolution took its toll on industrial Scotland, and by 1997 the Conservatives were unable to secure a single Scottish parliamentary seat.

In the meantime the Scottish National Party had become a serious political organisation, and argued effectively that the 'theft' of 'Scotland's oil', by Conservative *and* Labour, made it clear that that the only Parliament that would ever serve Scotland's interest was a Scottish one. New Labour offered a concession that still left the party with Scottish constituencies providing for a Westminster majority: a devolved Scottish Parliament within the United Kingdom. This provision made due acknowledgement that, unlike Ireland and Wales, Scotland had a history as a sovereign state; while yet ensuring that it would not separate. So it seemed.

At the time, many argued that the 'solution' was untenable: philosophically, culturally, psychologically and politically. Parliaments make national law and approve tax and expenditure. The Scottish parliament is restricted in its law-making powers and operates within the framework of an annual grant from the Treasury in London. Parliaments are part of the framework of established national institutions, and Scotland has its own legal and university systems dating from the middle ages, and its own Churches pre- and post-dating the reformation. Inevitably these now look to Holyrood rather than to Westminster, and are frustrated to be told that policy has to accord with London.

Invite an acute and sceptical people to celebrate the restoration of autonomy and they are likely to check that the terms of the settlement allow for home rule. Inevitably, since it involved a parliament but not sovereignty, the devolution settlement is more than the regional government provided for in Wales and Northern Ireland, but less than self-government, which is what the Scots, like the English, once had, and what they seem to want again.

New Labour practice was never in keeping with the character of Scotland. It is often said that Thatcher was uniquely unpopular north of the border; but the Conservatives faded faster under Ted Heath, while Thatcher stimulated the traditional Scots taste for prudence and independence among younger more radical conservatives. Certainly the late Donald Dewar, the cerebral cabinet minister charged with delivering Scottish devolution was well liked at home; but for all the talk of restoring community the Blairite embrace of recreational individualism and lifestyle liberalism appealed to very few.

Scotland combines pockets of real poverty and deprivation with a strong sense of proud history; marries a democratic intellectualism to an elitism of excellence; and links radicalism over social justice with respect for traditional values. Old Labour in the political heartland of Strathclyde and the West demanded economic redistribution in order that the poor should have the material means to enjoy the traditional domestic and cultural opportunities available to the middle-class.

The Scots radicals had little time for life-style liberalism. Often coming from Presbyterian, Roman Catholic or Episcopal backgrounds they viewed sexual promiscuity and abortion not as choices to be defended but as problems to be addressed. The late Cardinal Winning of Glasgow was very much in this tradition and Cardinal O'Brien of St Andrews and Edinburgh is increasingly identifying himself with it. It is no accident that resistance to liberalisation over same-sex relationships, including civil partnership and gay adoption has been more public and more marked north of the border and been lead by figures from working class backgrounds.

Gordon Brown's efforts to seem at ease with New Labour's social liberalism are unconvincing. The Pink News Website reported that he never attended a Parliamentary vote on gay rights issues since Labour came to power. At the same time he speaks with pride of his Christian formation, of the example of his father the Rev. John Brown minister of St Brycedale's Church in Kirkaldy during his son's formative years, and of the values and purposes of the Christian Socialist Movement. He has also taken to praising the social teaching of the Catholic Church saying that 'it was Pope Paul VI who set out, for our generation, the obligations that we all have a duty to meet: obligations that arise from — as he said in his own words — our mutual solidarity; the claims of social justice; and universal charity'. On his second visit to the Vatican, in 2007, he had the chance to speak with Pope Benedict XVI and presented him with *A Time to Serve*, a volume of his father's sermons.

Brown is a moral and intellectual heavyweight. Those qualities put him at ease among the Scots but have put strain on his relations with many in New Labour, and contribute to an impression of dour Scottishness that is unwelcome in the fun-loving, property-acquiring, free-living world depicted in media visions of New Britain — though a world now threatened by credit debt and negative equity.

The Scots are discontent with the halfway house of devolution; and the prime minister recognises the damage done to the Labour cause in Scotland by the promotion there of New Labour metropolitan liberalism. Being a genuine believer in Britain he is loath to yield to the demands for independence, but even the lesser condition of devolution poses a direct threat to him via the challenge presented by the West Lothian issue. This precisely mirrors the old Irish question: how can non-English MPs properly vote on English bills? In Brown's case the constitutional issue is deepened by the fact that his own constituents in Fife are mostly regulated by the Holyrood Parliament, while as PM he oversees policies for England and has prime ministerial accountability to Westminster for them, though he lacks an English electoral mandate.

Gladstone's solution in 1893 was to bar Irish MPs from voting on English Bills. It failed and in due course Ireland sought independence. Gordon Brown became Prime Minister in the weeks following the May 2007 election to the Scottish Parliament in which the Nationalists came to power. Being in a minority, for now, the SNP is unable to pass legislation for a referendum on Scottish independence. But the other parties have seen that a real political change has occurred and they are talking about more extensive devolution. That, however, will broaden and deepen the constitutional fracture and may further weaken the Union. And should the Scots withdraw from the UK, Ulster will not be far behind. Scottish monarchists can take some hope, however, from the thought that since the union of the parliaments came a century after that of the crowns they are constitutionally separate; hence the latter may survive the dissolution of the former, and the Queen might continue to rule as Elizabeth I of Scotland.

Six

Making Sense of Humanity

A marked feature of recent times is the sense of an increasing number of moral problems and ethical dilemmas. In part this is due to the decline in the influence of traditional morality which provided a framework of norms and requirements adequate to deal with most aspects of life. That it was able to do so is hardly surprising since it had been developed over many centuries during which the circumstances and challenges had changed relatively little. Nuclear war might threaten the prospect of mass destruction, but large scale slaughter had long been practised and the doctrine of just war was already ancient by the time of the First World War. Yet even those who hold fast to traditional morality must recognise that issues have arisen which could not possibly have been conceived of, even in the earlier parts of this century. Prominent among these are questions raised by science and technology.

Contemporary science is fast closing the gap between imagination and reality. From antiquity, men had dreamt of travelling through the sky and beneath the oceans; of journeying to the moon and of recreating the power of the sun. In this century these dreams have been realised, and the rate of achievement is accelerating. We are already familiar with organ transplants, key-hole surgery, micro-computers, mobile phones and palm-held media players, and each year brings new wonders. Increasingly, however, science and technology are generating philosophical and ethical problems.

Earlier generations knew of the dilemmas associated with nuclear research. On the one hand it had the capacity to provide a relatively cheap and long-term energy source, on the other it made possible new weapons of mass destruction and threatened lethal pollution. More recently, however, the focus of attention has shifted somewhat from the pros and cons of technology to the potential for science to change the way we think about human beings — and, indeed, to change their very nature.

The first significant challenge from science to traditional ideas of 'Man' came from Darwin's speculations in *The Origin of Species*. Prior to that the prevailing idea was of a hierarchy of fixed species with *homo sapiens* set apart from the rest of nature by its capacity for reason and moral consciousness; literally or metaphorically the offspring of Adam and Eve. The possibility that our rationality, along with our upright posture and sparsity of body hair, might be the result of natural selection resulting in 'descent with modification' from apes was deeply disturbing to the Victorians. In due course, though, an accommodation between theology and evolution was reached at least among the reflective. The late Pope John Paul II acknowledged the explanatory power of evolutionary science to the extent of saying that 'the theory of evolution is more than a hypothesis'. And in one of his last books *Rocks of Ages: Science and Religion in the Fullness of Life* (2001), the late Stephen Jay Gould proposed the idea of non-overlapping magisteria ('Noma'), with science explaining the material structure of the world, and religion addressing the matter of its meaning.

The spread of knowledge has made us less innocent than the Victorians, and our degree of pluralism, and relativism, means we are used to compartmentalising ideas and values. Nonetheless, we too should feel challenged by current scientific enquiry into aspects of human nature. In particular, it is difficult to over-estimate the potential impact of genetic research. This has two aspects. First, it raises questions

about what it is to be human and whether, for example, if we
are aggregations of genes, each determining some phenotypical trait including mental and behavioural ones, we can
possibly be free agents. Second, it introduces possibilities of
modifying features and of creating human beings by
genetic engineering.

Clearly there are potential benefits of genetic research,
and some forms of derived therapeutic treatment already
exist. But there are also dangers. In some cases we know the
likely bad effects of genetic mutation; in others we do not,
and these are perhaps most to be feared. What nature has
taken millions of years to effect should not lightly be inter-
fered with. A propensity to infection is something to be
dealt with, but simply eliminating it in an individual or in
a population may create further and greater problems.
There is evidently need here for careful analysis and wise
judgement.

Asked how he would act in certain circumstances Dr
Johnson replied 'sir, I know not what I *would do* but I know
what I *should do*'. Some genetic researchers may be inclined
to think that the only relevant principle is 'if it could be done,
then it should be done'. It would be foolish and morally
irresponsible to follow this rule, but it is no easy matter to
say what ethical principles should govern science and its
applications. Hence the need of wide-ranging public and
professional discussion, and again this is part of the case for
a national bioethics committee including scientists, medical
practitioners, ethicists, policy specialists, and user-group
representatives .

Initial advances in reproductive technology proved morally troublesome but they did not themselves challenge the
idea of human nature: for whether conceived within or
outside the womb, and whether developed from donated or
innately-endowed eggs, the baby itself remains a product of
nature. More threatening are developments in molecular
biology that offer the prospect of controlling physical and
psychological attributes by modifying underlying genetic
structures. And where gene-manipulation is impossible, or

too late to effect, there is the possibility of 'selection and termination' based on genetic screening. These possibilities have given rise to the idea of designer babies and to fears of increased abortion, and even of eugenics.

The evident presupposition of the research is that there is a systematic relation between genetic structure and manifest human characteristics: the genotypical determining the phenotypical. Expressed in the commonly favoured style, this is to say that there are (or may be) genes 'for' health, height, intelligence, musicality, sexuality, and so on. Discussion of these matters is apt to be confused. For example, health depends greatly on circumstance and no genetic endowment could eliminate environmental risks. Additionally, it is questionable whether the relation between genes and expressed characteristics is deterministic: having a propensity to some condition does not imply that one will actually suffer it. Also very few conditions appear to be monogenetically grounded; instead they result from a combination of genetic features plus environmental triggers and reinforcements.

One of the most sensitive areas of genetic research is that of psychology, in particular mental health, for this bears directly on our sense of human beings as persons, or to use an older vocabulary, as 'souls'. The fact that these subjects are sensitive and complex makes the need for public understanding and ethical reflection all the more important. Recognising this, in 1996 the UK Nuffield Council for Bioethics convened a Working Party to examine the then current state of knowledge and practice in the area of genetics and mental disorders, and to consider ethical, social and legal issues arising from this. Under the chairmanship of Dame Fiona Caldecott (Principal of Somerville College, Oxford and Past President of the Royal College of Psychiatrists) this worked for nearly two years to produce its report *Mental Disorders and Genetics: The Ethical Context*.

As a member of the Working Party I was struck from the outset by the ethical and philosophical issues it faced, and given their importance I have not been surprised by the very considerable press coverage of the report following its publication. Here I wish to draw attention to three issues that we confronted and which are of general relevance when thinking about the implications of genetic research. First, there is the need to avoid *geneticisation*; second, there is the necessity of identifying appropriate *norms and values*; and third, there is the concern with *stigmatisation*.

Two perspectives on human beings are relevant in this context. First, that from the micro-physical base *up* through various strata (chemical and anatomical) to the level of whole functioning intelligent organisms: *persons*. Second, that from the level of personal existence *down* through the sub-personal to the physico-chemical basis. In relation to these it is possible to distinguish two kinds of priority. It *might* be that the behaviour of persons is to be wholly accounted in terms of the matter out of they are composed, that is to say the material base might be *constitutively prior*. At the same time, however, the proper object of ethical concern is the condition of the whole human being, i.e. the person is *ethically prior*.

Since we are concerned with ethical issues, the relevant order of priority is one favouring persons; and so the proper perspective is that in which the genetic base is viewed through its effects at the personal level. In short, we should be primarily concerned with *people* and not with their genes. Additionally, the current state of philosophical thinking about the nature of things psychological is anti-reductionist. That is to say, while most philosophers believe in the material basis of the mind they do not suppose that psychology is reducible to a physical science. Rather they subscribe to the idea that the psychological aspect of human nature is an emergent or supervenient level of reality with its own structures and principles of operation. As well as being of theoretical interest this conclusion provides an obstacle to scientistic approaches to human psychology.

Relatedly, philosophy and the social sciences maintain that personhood is expressed and developed in the context of interaction with others. Thought is intimately connected with language, and this is essentially social. More particularly, the term 'I' can only be applied by a being that has the idea of others and the capacity to view him or herself as an object of attention for others. No other, no self; no linguistic community, no language development; no language, no thought; no society, no person. Given these dependencies the geneticist idea that persons and their psychologies might be reduced to genes is incoherent. *Geneticisation* is an error that can and should be resisted.

Turning to norms and values, these fall within two broad categories. First, there are those relating to welfare — in the present context mainly limiting harm and suffering. Second, are those concerned with respect for human beings and for their dignity. The former are expressed in efforts to cure, to care and not to injure. The latter are shown by giving due weight to personal autonomy and integrity, and in recognising the obligations of doctors and researchers to seek consent and to respect privacy and confidentiality. In the case of the mentally defective or disordered these latter norms are hard to implement; but they must not be abandoned, nor set aside in the name of the 'best interests' of the individual or of the community. Persons must be respected.

Finally there is the issue of *stigmatisation*. Physical injuries and illnesses rarely bring shame or blame to sufferers or their families; yet those afflicted with mental disorder may have to suffer not only their disease but also the associated stigma (as may their relatives). Of its nature, research into the genetic foundations of mental disorder may increase the stigma associated with it, and hence increase the prevalence of abortion. For the most part, however, stigma results not from experience of difficult behaviour by the mentally disordered but from the ignorance and misconceptions of others about the nature of mental illness. These attitudes are evidence of lack of understanding, lack of sympathy and lack of respect for fellow human beings.

Again I emphasise the importance and ineliminability of humanity. Our genes may be important but they are not the arbiter of personhood, nor are they the foundation of human value. Humanity is an irreducible status and an inescapable duty. Persons are persons, first and foremost — and, as I shall argue in the next chapter, human persons are constituted and survive as such from their conception to their death. Curiously there is a symmetry between the modern scientistic error that would reduce persons to their matter, and in the old spiritualist one that would deny that they we are essentially bodily beings. Humanity is material in composition but moral in nature.

Seven

Respecting Life: Ethics and Embryos

Moral philosophy begins with moral intuitions and then, by arguments, either confirms or refutes them. There was a time when it was not thought to be so. For, until recently it was assumed that philosophers ought not, as philosophers, to concern themselves with actual moral problems, but should instead only analyse the language of ethics. Those bad days are gone, and a mark of their passing is the frequent involvement of philosophers in the public debate of social and moral issues.

One very widespread moral intuition is the sense that it is always wrong to kill the innocent. Can this be given a rational defence? Suppose we are interested in moral truth and are neither sceptics nor nihilists; then it is evident that the prohibition against murder will be a part of any acceptable ethical system. A moral view that countenanced the taking of innocent life would be corrupt but also incoherent. What could it offer as a higher value to be aimed at in preference to respect for life? Possibly the achievement of one's well-being whatever the cost to others?—or perhaps the preservation of the species? But the former could only be self-defeating, since with each concerned to further his or her own good there could be no possibility of the safety and stability necessary for the realisation and maintenance of individual well-being. The ethics of species-preservation suffers from a similar kind of incoherence. For it is quite clear, particularly in the modern world, that the only hope of saving human kind is by a policy built upon respect for individual human life.

The same point can be brought against those who would elevate a political ideal, be it formed in terms of the *state*, the *nation* or a *class*, above the prohibition against murder. The belief that one may kill the innocent, for whatever reason, is morally repugnant, but also self-defeating with respect to whatever other value is given priority. One who urges that it is acceptable to act in this way is unlikely to live to see the kind of society he wants; nor could such a society be expected to survive; since from its very moment of conception it would be vulnerable to the activities of those who like its architects adhere to a doctrine of justified murder.

Beyond the basic intuition that innocent life ought to be respected, and the pragmatic defence of that principle, many believe that the prohibition on intentionally destroying the innocent rests on a deeper foundation. Indeed this prohibition may be grounded in a variety of ways. Some invoke Divine commands recorded in scripture; others, influenced by the Graeco-Roman tradition of natural law may say that human beings are intrinsically valuable, and that that among the worst (natural) evils that a human can suffer is to lose its life. Hence, to inflict this loss upon it is to do it a very great wrong. Others speak about the existential value of human life, the community of fellow humans, and so on, and claim that there is a 'familial' or social duty of respect towards the lives of the innocent. Obviously these views differ but it is significant that a wide variety of religious and secular moralities maintain in common a prohibition against the taking of innocent human life.

Of course, this consensus may be, and indeed is challenged; but in my experience when such challenges are made it is worth asking who it is the challengers want it to be permissible to kill: foetuses, incapacitated infants, civilian populations, the terminally ill, the senile? Human life is not always pretty, happy or convenient, but if it has any intrinsic value that is not diminished by circumstance.

Ethical intuition and prudential reasoning are in agreement in rejecting the view that it is sometimes permissible to commit wilful murder for the sake of some desired, and even desirable, end. This conclusion bears directly on a number of current issues concerning, for example, terrorist violence, the possible use of weapons of mass destruction. the practice of terminating a pregnancy, and certain forms of stem cell research. I am here concerned with the last two of these issues.

Consider first, abortion. The argument against terminating life in the womb is an application of the principle mentioned above:

1. It is always wrong to take the life of an innocent human being.

2. A foetus in the womb is an innocent human being.

3. Therefore, it is always wrong to take the life of a foetus.

Since the reasoning is valid, the conclusion can only be rejected by denying one or both of the premises. As regards (1) however, the cost of denying it is a lessening of respect for life, and thereby a weakening of the argument against terrorism and unjust wars. The case against chemical or nuclear warfare is not merely one of quantity, as if killing a thousand people was wrong though killing one or two was not; and even if it were, the staggering total of abortions rivals the 'Megadeath' figures calculated by military strategists.

The other and more popular option for the defender of abortion is to deny (2). Typically it is claimed that human beings exhibit certain species characteristics, e.g., thought, deliberation and language use, and that since a foetus lacks such capacities therefore it cannot be classed as one of these. The central flaw in this reasoning is its equivocation on the meaning of 'capability'. *To be capable* may mean either: currently able to do a thing, or potentially able to do it, i.e., to be the sort of creature that can engage in the activity. While a foetus may (in the first sense) be incapable of thought, it may yet belong to a species of thinking animals. Incapacity in its former meaning no more disqualifies it from being a human subject than does senility or imbecility remove an individual from the human race. A human is not as such a foetus, an infant, a young man or an old man. Rather these are proper stages in the development of life. I shall return to this matter when considering stem cell research, but for the moment conclude that there is no good reason to deny that a foetus is a human being that is not also a reason for denying that an infant or an adult is. To follow the case for abortion in this direction leads easily to an apparent justification of infanticide and non-voluntary euthanasia.

As before, it will be as well to anticipate and respond to objections. The first will come from those who argue that anti-abortion legislation forces women to procure miscarriages in circumstances and by means which are likely to lead to more deaths not fewer. This concern to eliminate the 'back-street abortion' is virtuous, but it simply fails to touch the present issue. If, as I maintain, abortion is unjustified killing then it is irrelevant in moral terms whether it is legal or illegal, and it is also beside the point whether the context is or is not that of a medically safe operation. Certainly unqualified terminations are dangerous and ought to be avoided for the sake of the mother, but all abortion is lethal and ought to be avoided for the sake of the innocent foetus. Let me add, however, that the adoption of this position obliges the defender of life to do what he or she can to enable women to bear unwanted pregnancies by removing stigmas attached to illegitimacy and handicaps, and by campaigning for proper assistance for those in need.

A different form of objection is that brought forward under the banner *A Woman's Right to Choose*. This charges that the question whether or not to have an abortion falls within a person's prerogative to decide how their body may be used. This is not the trivial claim that each person has the right to choose how to act. This, though true, is independent of issues of rightness or wrongness in behaviour — for in this sense a person has the *right* to do wrong. Rather the claim is that an unwanted pregnancy is an infringement of a property right, and that the woman's entitlement to determine the use of her body overrides the right of the foetus not to be killed.

This argument has several aspects but it will be sufficient to note two points. First, suppose we allow the (contentious) claim that an unwanted pregnancy constitutes the violation of a property right. It is surely an error to believe that this proprietorial claim licences the killing of an innocent human being. To suppose otherwise is to fall in with those challenged earlier who elevate some other feature above the right to life and who in consequence put at risk their preferred value. Second and relatedly, property rights are conditional upon the maintenance of life. Without full respect for the latter the former are reduced to a set of accidental facts of possession lacking any moral justification. In short, the right of the innocent not to be killed is fundamental to any coherent conception of human rights and is the basis for any further claims.

With these considerations in place let me turn next to the matter of stem cell research. I am unable to do justice here to the range and variety of issues involved in the question of human stem cell research but I hope at least to clarify some points on which there is no small degree of confusion. Clarity by itself is insufficient to resolve the issues, but they will certainly not be resolved adequately without it, and in my experience there is a good deal of muddled thinking not least among those involved in conducting such research.

Setting aside the possibility of using adult stem cells in ways that do *not* involve implanting them in human eggs evacuated of their nuclei for the purpose, which is itself ethically problematical, I shall confine myself to the case, which is currently that of greatest concern, namely, the use of stem cells derived from human embryos, though the main points carry over to many other cases.

There is one issue above all others that we need to get clear about: the status of the human embryo at its earliest stage of formation. Someone might agree that the life of an innocent human being commands respect and ought never

intentionally to be destroyed; but they may claim that an
early embryo is not a human being. It may be *human*, in the
sense that some material is human rather than cat tissue, but
that does not make it *a human*. Here we come again to the
philosophical issue of the nature of what is produced in
conception.

In human sexual reproduction, two *gametes* (sperm and
ovum) come together to produce a new entity a *zygote*. After
a short period that new creation will implant itself in the
wall of the womb, and if there are no faults or failures it will
develop over the coming months and then be born. That
will not happen if there is some natural impediment, or if
the process is artificially blocked, or if the new creation is
destroyed.

Stem cell research of the sort I am concerned with
involves destroying the early embryo — the blastocyst. This
is not in dispute. What is contested, by some, is whether
those embryos are human beings. In a recent book, *After
Dolly: The Uses and Misuses of Cloning* (2006), for example,
Ian Wilmut discusses the ethical disputes and offers his
own account of the status of the human blastocyst.

He rightly corrects the impression that conception is an
instantaneous event involving fusion of sperm and egg. As
he observes, gamete fusion is part of a process leading to the
production of an entity with a distinct genetic identity. Nevertheless, that process is rapidly achieved, and thereafter
embryonic development is in accord with the DNA of the
new individual.

Dr Wilmut remarks that the self-developing early
embryo 'is a far cry from the popular image ... of a little foetus with limbs and heart. Nor would I think of babies when I
gaze at a human blastocyst'. Yet the varying appearance of
an organism at different developmental stages gives no
reason to doubt that what is present is one and the same
individual. Indeed, the concept of developmental phases
presupposes this. Next, he invokes the idea that because the
blastocyst is an individual human something with 'the
potential to become a person ... that does not mean that it is

a person, just as a young girl who wants to study medicine is not a qualified doctor'. This is a familiar move parallel to the claim that just because an acorn becomes an oak tree that does not make it one now. It is, however, confused.

Distinguish two uses of a term such as 'oak' 'cat' or 'human' (being or person): one is *generic*, saying what kind of being something is (*quercus, felis, homo*), the other is *phasic*, describing a phase or stage in its life. Now consider the claim 'because an acorn or a kitten has the potential to become an oak or a cat, respectively, it does not follow that they are ones already'. That is true if by 'oak' or 'cat' is meant the mature or adult phase; but of course in the other and more relevant generic sense an acorn is certainly an oak (an individual *quercus*) and a kitten is certainly a cat (an individual *felis*). The young girl is not an adult doctor, but adult and child are both human beings. Embryo, foetus, baby, infant, child, youth, and adult are phases in the life career of a human.

Likewise, for potentiality: distinguish the potential for a human to come into existence, from the potential for developed human activity that is present in virtue of already being human. Egg and sperm are the principle components of the former, and the blastocyst constitutes the realisation of that potential. An embryo is not a potential human being but a human being with potential. To destroy it is to kill a human being; and if such killing is wrong in general then it is wrong in the case where the blastocyst is destroyed for stem cell research. As with terminating a pregnancy one is inescapably confronted with the issue of killing an innocent human being, and it is hard to see how that can be justified without giving up a belief that is central and foundational within human morality more generally.

Eight

Respecting Life: Ethics and Waging War

In the previous chapter I was concerned with the extermination of human life in its early stages of development, and I argued that if one believes that innocent human life ought never intentionally to be destroyed then one ought to regard the deliberate destruction of human embryos and foetuses as a grave moral wrong. Interestingly opponents of this view are often vehement in their opposition to the killing of innocents in war, regarding this, rightly I believe, as a great moral evil. Here I leave it to them to address the apparent tension in their views and move on to consider how the principle of respecting the innocent bears upon the conduct of warfare.

As the prospect of a second Gulf War came ever closer during the close of 2002 and in the early months of 2003 those arguing in favour of launching an assault on the forces of Saddam Hussein shifted their ground from appealing to the fear of an Iraqi sponsored or aided terrorist attack upon Western cities, to invoking the broad demands of justice. Indeed the official website later established by the Multi National Force carried the title *Operation Iraqi Freedom*. The move from talk of 'self-interest' to that of other-regarding 'duty' was significant as a piece of political rhetoric and because it will be in terms of these contrasting ideas that what took place that spring and summer will come to be judged by history.

Whereas a pre-emptive strike was first said to be prudent, and next morally permissible, it was then proposed by Tony Blair, Colin Powell, George W. Bush and Jack Straw, and by a few others, to be close to morally obligatory. The suggestion was that if an anti-Iraqi military alliance did not confront this issue, then its members would have failed in their duties of protection to their own citizens, to the people of Iraq, to the Kurds, to the populations of the wider middle East (most especially the Israelis and the Palestinians, both) and to the peoples of the world.

This was an interesting turning of the moral case against those who had been vociferous in opposing the very idea of war; and to judge from the comments of some religious leaders in Britain, such as Archbishop Mario Conti and the Chief Rabbi Jonathan Sacks, the case was not without its sympathisers among those professionally concerned with the morality of public policies. In speaking out against the anticipated invasion of Iraq the Archbishops of Westminster and Canterbury cited the doctrine of 'Just War', but as that expression suggests this idea can be invoked to show that war is permissible and even obligatory, as well as to show that it is prohibited.

Rabbi Sacks observed that the campaign against Iraq must have 'clear and achievable aims, must be supported by a broad international coalition, and all possible precautions must be taken to prevent civilian casualties'. He added that the world should reflect on the Israeli air force's attack on Iraq's Osirak nuclear reactor in 1981. This was widely criticised at the time but was subsequently seen to have been critical in delaying Sadam's Hussein's acquisition of nuclear weapons. Not unreasonably, Sacks claimed that 'if not for that air attack, the world would today be facing a virtually impossible situation' (meaning, I presume, nuclear blackmail with the likely prospect of Israeli retaliation).

Likewise Archbishop Conti reasoned from the traditional conditions of just war to the conclusion that US/UK threats of attack might well be justified: 'my reply to the question of whether the [current] threat of force could be justified was clear. If the threat is necessary to make the regime of Saddam Hussein comply with international law; if the menace of severe repercussions is needed to disarm a brutal dictator who has launched programmes of genocide against his own people; then yes, such threats can be justified'.

Archbishop Conti prefaced his judgement by observing 'I have been somewhat surprised that so many people of all faiths and of none have seized on this doctrine [of just war] and made it their own in recent weeks, though I am content that they recognise the wisdom of the Church in developing a sensible set of criteria for judging the appropriateness or otherwise of military action'.

Given the origins of the doctrine of just war in Catholic moral theology it is indeed ironic to see it so widely invoked in a secularised society generally preoccupied with the wrongs inflicted by Christianity in general (the customary examples are 'the crusades' and 'the inquisition') and by the Roman Church in particular. For all that, however, we are now likely to hear much more about what just war does and does not sanction, and it may be useful, therefore, to offer a brief review of this piece of Catholic doctrine.

In 324 AD/CE, following a victory at the battle of Chrysopolis, Constantine became sole Emperor, uniting the Roman Empire and establishing a new second imperial capital in Byzantium, thereafter 'Constantinople' until its fall in 1453 after which it was renamed by the Ottomans 'Istanbul'. His conversion to Christianity put an end to three centuries of persecution, and resulted in its becoming the official religion of the Empire. Christians then had to think about their loyalties; and as the Empire came under attack from the 'Goths' they were forced to consider the question of whether it was morally permissible to take up arms— though there had already been some number of Christians in the Roman army from the second century. The fall of Rome in 410 made this matter more urgent and so began a tradition of reflection on the conditions under which it might be permissible to go to war. Authors such as St Augustine (354–430) in the fifth century, and St Thomas

Aquinas (1225–74) in the late middle ages contributed to this theory of just war. In the *Summa Theologiae* (1271) Aquinas sets three conditions 'in order for a war to be just':

> First, the authority of the sovereign [*auctoritas principis*] by whose command the war is to be waged. For … the care of the common good is committed to those who are in authority, it is their business to watch over the good of the city, kingdom or province subject to them. And just as it is lawful for them to have recourse to the sword in defending that common good against internal disturbances … so too, it is their business to have recourse to the sword of war in defending the common good against external enemies.
>
> Second, a just cause [*justa causa*] is required, namely that those who are attacked, should be attacked because they deserve it on account of some fault …
>
> Third, it is necessary that the belligerents should have a rightful intention [*recta intentio*], so that they intend the advancement of good, or the avoidance of evil. Hence Augustine says 'True religion regards as just those wars that are waged not for motives of aggrandisement, or cruelty, but with the object of securing peace, of punishing evil-doers, and of uplifting the good.'

Subsequently, the theory was most extensively developed in the sixteenth and seventeenth centuries. The work was done mostly in Spain and Portugal, parts of the world that had good reason to reflect on the rights and wrongs of warring with other nations and peoples. Still relatively little known is the figure of Bartolome de Las Casas (1484–1576) the 'Apostle of the Indies'. His father sailed with Columbus, but Bartolome spent much of his own life arguing for the rights of native peoples of the New World where he himself was the first ordained priest. In his work *Destruccion de las Indias* he wrote powerfully and in detail about the abuse of the Amerindians. Given his vocation as a preacher, subsequent to having been trained as a lawyer, it is especially significant that in 1548 he opposed in public debate the claim that 'wars may be waged against the infidels in order to prepare the way for preaching the faith'.

The following year was born, in Granada, Francisco Suarez (1548–1617) who became a Jesuit and is widely regarded as the founder of International Law. In his work *On the Theological Virtues* Suarez maintains the following: 'the first heresy is the claim that it is intrinsically evil and contrary to charity to wage war … in itself war is not intrinsically evil, nor is it forbidden to Christians to wage it. War is not opposed to the love of one's enemies; for whoever wages war honourably hates not individuals but the evil actions he justly punishes'.

Out of Suarez's writings and those of his contemporaries comes the following list of seven conditions of 'Just War':

1. The war must be made by a lawful authority.

2. The war must be waged for a morally just cause.

3. The warring state must have a rightful intention, i.e. to pursue the just cause.

4. The war must be the only means of achieving the just end.

5. There must be a reasonable prospect of victory.

6. The goods to be achieved must be greater than the probable evil effects of waging war.

7. The means of war must not themselves be evil: either by being such as to cause gratuitous injuries or deaths, or by involving the intentional killing of innocent civilians.

Whatever may now be said on either side of the argument about the second Gulf war, at the time it was no trivial matter to determine whether what was planned by Bush and Blair was likely to satisfy these criteria. Some claimed that the stated intentions were not the real purpose and that the true aims were selfish ones, having to do with ensuring oil supplies. Whatever the truth about that, however, it was hard to suppose that the war was the only means of achieving the avowed just cause, or that the goods to be achieved would be greater than the evil effects.

As it is, the whole affair has been a disaster and has done great damage to the moral standing of the allied powers, in particular America. Politicians make much of the idea that

they are concerned with practical strategies aimed at securing real benefits, and that hair-splitting scholastic theories
have little to contribute to this. Ironically, however, had the
scholastic doctrine of just war been better known and
attended to, it might well have been that an artefact of mediaeval ethical theory would have inhibited contemporary
consequentialist strategies of war, and saved our leaders
from incurring harms to their own people as well as inflict-
ing terrible and longstanding suffering upon the people of
Iraq.

I began by making a connection between the theme of the
previous chapter and that of the present one, and suggested
a tension in the views of those who readily defend abortion
and embryo destruction for the sake of greater benefit,
while yet denouncing the destruction of innocent civilians.
But the most common justification for doing the latter is that
is serves the overall interest, which is likewise the most
common defence of destroying life in its beginnings. Little
surprise, then, that politicians assume that the populace is
utilitarian in outlook and rely upon that assumption in
making policy. This gives reason to think it may be true that
we get the leaders we deserve.

Nine

A Union of Communities

Over the last twenty years I have had the opportunity to visit the United States many times, and even to live there for two periods: for a few months of 1987 in Pittsburgh, and for the 2001–02 academic year in the area of Washington DC. In 2006 I was in the US on four occasions: first, in Los Angeles to discuss whether the philosophy of Wittgenstein brings to an end the traditional preoccupations of metaphysics; second, in Boston to discuss the philosophical ideas of the late Pope John Paul II; third to speak about the nature of thought to a conference in Ohio; and fourth to lecture and speak in Washington DC and in New York. The point of mentioning these various intellectual purposes will become clear.

The contrasts between the first two visits were striking. California was bathed in heat untypical even of the golden state; Massachusetts was emerging falteringly from bitter snowstorms that had frozen transport to a halt. The climatic difference between one coast and another is familiar enough, but the evidently increasing gap is being widely cited as further evidence of global warming. It is one thing to hear reports of this from faraway parts; it is quite another when two such iconic states, representing the wealth and achievements of old and new America, seem directly affected.

In the preceding weeks Evangelical Christian leaders had joined liberal humanist voices in calling for government action to control 'human-induced climate change', and the word from the Whitehouse was that it is listening. In his 2006 State of the Union address President G.W. Bush spoke of the US as being 'addicted to oil', which in a society troubled by substance abuse carries an echo of familiar warnings against self-destruction. Late and slow as this response may be, it is a sign of a national 'awakening', recalling the great religious stirring of the nineteenth century. Ironically, the evangelical tone of American political rhetoric, of which Europeans often complain, may yet prove to be a cause of the environmental salvation they seek.

Los Angeles and Boston, like other major American cities, are united by their intense and widespread interest in education and ideas. This introduces a further contrast, which is between America and Britain. There are several common opinions about the US by which the British flatter themselves as to their political and cultural superiority. One is that Americans are possessive individualists with no proper sense of society. Another is that they are naively materialistic, preferring work and acquisition to relaxed enjoyment of the sufficiencies of life. A third is that they favour the new over the old and the practical over the abstract. A fourth is that America lacks history and so is without cultural and intellectual foundations. Putting these together in a 'view', it amounts to an image of the US as individualistic, materialistic, pragmatic and culturally free-floating.

These characteristics will be found, as will their exact opposites. But the general truth about America is that it is far more authentically communitarian, idealistic and respectful of history than is Britain. Of course the US is a modern polity, but its institutional history is now four centuries old. West and east provide contrasting examples of this. In the south-west, a chain of mission settlements was established along the San Antonio River in New Mexico from 1690, and in the next century twenty further missions were created along six hundred miles of the Californian coast from Sonoma to San Diego. In Florida, the Spanish established the fortress town of St Augustine in 1565, whose remaining bastions recall those of Valetta. These accomplishments mark the influence of Spanish Catholic culture, which has been reinvigorated in recent times by ongoing Hispanic immigration.

In the north-east, meanwhile, preparations were advanced for the 400th anniversary in 2007 of James VI/I grants of land (in Virginia and New England) to London and Plymouth companies. The first peace treaty with the Indians came in 1621, and following a further grant (from Charles I) the significant settlements began in 1630. By 1635 the Boston Latin school had been established, and in 1636 the Puritans founded a university, later named after John Harvard who bequeathed it land and books.

This creation occurred when Galileo, Hobbes, Rubens, and Bernini were alive, and before the birth of Newton, Leibniz, and William of Orange. Following the establishment of Edinburgh University in 1583 it took the British 250 years to found their next university (Durham, 1832), but in the meantime the Americans had established a further forty or so, including William and Mary (1693), St John's (1696), Yale (1701), Princeton (1746), Pennsylvania (1757), Columbia (1754), and Georgetown (1789).

These served the practical purpose of training for leadership, but as important was their work of moral and cultural formation. Due in large part to Scottish influence the Americans acquired the reputation, which they still deserve, for being people of ideas. In a work widely read in the US, but little known in Britain, the French aristocrat Alexis de Tocqueville wrote in 1831 of his favourable impression of the Americans: 'without ever having taken the trouble to define the rules of a philosophical method, they are in possession of one common to the whole people ...' (*Democracy in America*). He was also the first to observe the American genius for forming thriving communities without the aid of political authority or direction.

The collectivist thinking that overtook Europe in the twentieth century committed the fallacy of identifying communities with the state. The assumption that Americans are anti-social individualists derives from this same error. Certainly they are suspicious of the claims of government; but that is precisely because they value real communities of family, neighbourhood, locality or common identity, and see these as threatened by bureaucrats and politicians. To anyone familiar with life on both sides of the Atlantic it is striking how in Britain every aspect of life is taken to permit, and even to require, political action. Believing in the value of real communities Americans strive to protect them from public ownership.

The flourishing of religion in America, and its failing in Europe, is related to these points. The constitutional prohibition on the establishment of religion was not a secularist policy but one devised to protect the religious liberty of all. A further benefit is that since church is not provided for, it has to be created, and sustained, by faith communities. In the UK, by contrast, the provision of religion is presumed to be a public service, like fresh water and healthcare, and not to be the responsibility of anyone but its official providers. But faith cannot survive, let alone flourish, unless it is rooted in common life.

Religion in America is also a force in the culture wars: abortion, stem-cell research, euthanasia, capital punishment, gay marriage, illegitimacy, etc, are more prominent in public debate than they are in Britain. The voice of social conservatism is also stronger, precisely because of the concern of families and communities to protect themselves from politically imposed values. Alongside religious notions, however, stand political, legal and philosophical thought. A visit to any large bookstore confirms America's love of ideas, ideals and argumentation. Whether at the journalistic or academic level the standards are enviable. Indeed, American universities now lead the world not only in science, technology and medicine, but in classics, history, cultural studies and philosophy.

So I return to the intellectual purposes of my first two visits. Wittgenstein in one way, and John Paul in another, appeal strongly to the American appetite for deep, serious and wide-ranging systems of thought. Both men were central Europeans, both were born into religious homes; both had a deep appreciation of the arts; both wrote in defence of the human world against the pressures of scientific reductionism; and both are now studied most intensely in America. Still today, US intellectuals look to Europe, but the era of dependence is over and in the comparison between cultures the judgement of seriousness and achievement must increasingly favour America. Criticism may be apt, but honour is due, and self-examination is necessary.

A later academic visit fell in the week before the congressional elections and I had time for a walk along Broadway. I had done the same in 2000 on the day of the Presidential election, and I recalled how returning to the US several weeks later, the outcome of the 'hanging-chad' poll had still been unresolved. There was some fear of further polling machine foul-ups in 2006, though in the event they were few and had no impact on the outcome.

Broadway looked unchanged even with the drain on the economy from the years of the Afghan and Iraq wars; and with Christmas in prospect the shop-fronts were twinkling all the brighter. It's an impressive sight to behold: Broadway, Granville Village, Licking County, Central Ohio.

The town is a model community settled in 1805 by New Englanders in search of fertile farming land. It was designed and built in swift order and soon began to flourish. Churches, schools and a college were founded, and canal and railroad connections established. It is a picture of well-groomed, small town America: white fences and porches, well-attended churches; library and local museums staffed by volunteers; first-name friendliness in stores and diners; an active historical association.

It is a realisation of a popular version of heaven on earth — like *The Truman Show* but old-time and without the deception. I stayed in the home of a couple who have restored their house to its Victorian condition and character, and secured its inclusion on the national register of historic places. My academic host is a committed teacher and scholar, an active member of the Democratic party, a main-stay of the local historical association, and an editor of the recent three-volume bi-centennial Granville history.

The idea and practice of good citizenship are as old as the republic itself. When de Tocqueville wrote about *Democracy in America* he observed that American towns 'are like great meeting houses with all the inhabitants as members', and that 'Americans of all ages, all stations of life, and all types of disposition are forever forming associations. ... In demo-cratic countries knowledge of how to combine is the mother of all other forms of knowledge; on its progress depends that of all the others.'

Whatever the real motives for the Iraq war, part of the rhetoric of persuasion appealed to the idea, natural to Americans, that those who had suffered tyranny deserved the chance to organise themselves in free democratic associ-ation. As it turns out, that ideal may not be universal; and the disaster of Iraq is plain to see. That, and evidence of corruption in state and national legislatures, cost the Republicans the election.

Ohio is the bellwether of American public opinion. In 2004 it had given the Presidency to Bush, but in 2006 it turned, giving the Democrats their first Governor for sixteen years with successes at other levels in state and nationally. The immediate result of the swing from the Republicans was talk of changing foreign policy but this is not, as such, a conservative/progressive issue.

The real questions for America concern domestic issues; and how they are resolved could affect the politics of Brit-ain. As senior Democrats from the North East prepared to resume the cause of liberal progressivism, others closer to the ground cautioned that it would be premature to sup-pose that this was an electoral defeat for conservatism. Indeed, where moderate conservatives stood, they won; but this time many of them were standing as Democrats — some even having changed parties.

In all probability the Bush presidency will be viewed as having failed multiply: failed in moving closer to a solution of the Israel/Palestine problem; failed in engaging moderate Islam; failed in laying the foundations for stability in Iraq; failed in dealing with Iran and North Korea; failed in developing co-operative strategies with China and Russia; failed in working out a positive relationship with continental Europe; failed in limiting the national debt; and failed in providing for Republican success in the mid-term elections, and in the Presidential one in 2008.

Left-wing Democrats ridicule the administration for its arrogance, aggression and stupidity. Right-wing Conservatives abuse it for its lack of courage, its evasiveness and its profligacy. Now that it has been turned against by the electorate at large, the severist critics are likely to be those on the right who see their hopes of rolling back the state broken on the wheel of Democratic governance; perhaps after 2008 with a straight line-up along Pennsylvania Avenue from Congress to the Whitehouse.

The American people, however, have showed no real sign of wanting a radical de-federation of the country. They have recognised, since the period of Roosevelt's 1930s New Deal programme, and his 1941 Congressional speech, that the 'four freedoms' he spoke of: 'freedom of speech and expression … freedom of every person to worship God in his own way … freedom from want … and freedom from fear', could only be secured by a strong federal government, deploying the resources of the nation as a whole, for the sake of all Americans, and, to some degree, for the sake of the world as a whole.

It is sometimes sneered that Americans stay at home and are ignorant of the world. It is worth remembering, however, that the country is the world's third largest by size and population; in area two and a half times that of the European Union, with 300 million people spread across six time zones. It has enormous natural resources and a varied and landscape honoured in the verses of *America the Beautiful*:

O beautiful for spacious skies,
For amber waves of grain,
For purple mountain majesties,
Above the fruited plain!

It is also the largest and most powerful economy in the
world; with a political structure that duplicates the federal
system in each of the fifty states—including fifty supreme
courts. America is more a continent than a country with
enough at home to fill its people's lives. Besides, just how
much do the British or the French know about the wider
world?

America has rejected libertarian attacks on the very idea
of federal government, neo-conservative foreign policy,
and fundamentalist intolerance. What it has not rejected,
however, is moderate social conservatism. Recent election
results favour that position, and Democrat national figures
who fail to register or overlook this could encourage the
election of a moderate Republican as President in 2008. But
the best evidence of America's social conservatism is
America itself—not the heights of Manhattan or of Los
Angeles as portrayed in TV series and films; but the America that begins twenty miles of the beltway west of Washington and continues all the way to the valleys inland from
the coastal cities of California. Not the Broadway of NYC,
but that of towns like Granville Ohio, which for all its
specialness is dulplicated again and again from sea to
shining sea.

Ten

Moral Tales

It is tempting to think of the *Toy Story* films as simplified but accurate reflections of contemporary American Society: garishly coloured, rather too loud, simple minded and sentimental, with manufactured goods taking the traditional place of human companions. Woody, Buzz, Potato Head and the other toys (plain or mutilated) may be the foreground characters, but behind them are the humans who own them.

With his skull T shirt, Sid (vicious?) is obviously something of a junior Dr Frankenstein cannibalising toys to create horrible hybrids, but there may also be personality problems in store for innocent Andy. In *Toy Story* mother is busy with other things and father is barely in evidence; all that Andy has, it seems, are his late twentieth century, mass-produced, wind-up or battery-operated friends. *We* know that they have lives of their own, but Andy does not; or at least if he does believe this then he may grow up hating humans, for they are likely to prove a disappointment to him. I would not be at all surprised if in a few years time some 'alternative' animators produce a film of Andy's psychopathic teenage years featuring virtual-reality sessions and shoot-outs at burger bars.

However, rather than view the *Toy Story* films as indicators of unqualified social decline and rising insanity I would like to offer another, and gentler, interpretation. Watching *Toy Story* again at Christmas with my four children my thoughts were carried back into the distant past. In the 6th century—thirteen hundred years before Walt Disney was born — Pope Gregory the Great initiated a series of reforms in the Western Christian Church. Among his accomplishments was the effective rejection of the idea that it was inappropriate for artists to depict episodes from the bible. Noting that 'painting can do for the illiterate what writing does for those who can read' Gregory encouraged the decoration of churches with vivid picture stories. So was born the educational cartoon.

Of late, there has been a trend to animate sacred text, *Prince of Egypt* is one such, though there are more pious and obviously religious productions available from small Christian production companies. But it is interesting to reflect for a moment on the parallels between traditional art and the computer-produced imagery of *Toy Story*. Renaissance painting began with the effort to render figures, buildings and landscapes in more naturalistic style. The likes of Giotto achieved this by using strong, clean colours, well-defined borders and sharp shadows. As well as making for bold imagery this served to render the scenes more vivid, and so encouraged viewers to enter into them as imagined participants. All of this being part of the attempt to impress ideas of good and evil, heaven and hell, on receptive minds.

The power of clear bold images to convey ideas is even more effective when worked upon children. That fact was familiar to the illustrators of traditional story books, and it lay behind Disney's deliberate development of colour animation as a way of conveying morally improving tales. Whether the idea was of 'gentle Jesus meek and mild' or of 'sweet Snow White neat and tidy', clear, clean figures served to impress the ideal. So it is with Woody, Buzz and the rest as they struggle against danger, misfortune and wrongdoing.

Part of the appeal of the *Toy Story* films, then, is that they present moral tales in images as clear as their plots. There are few if any shades of grey, morally or literally, and that provides a comfortable retreat from the real world. The Americans, the British and other English-language peoples have a particular fondness for children's' tales. This reflects, I think, the value we place on childhood and our wish never to leave it too far behind us even as we grow older. The family film is a peculiarly Anglo-American category and *Toy Story I* and *II* certainly fall within it.

Like pantomimes they have something for everyone: slapstick humour, thrills and spills, romance, and witty asides for the benefit of the adults. They also make knowing references to other styles of film and television: Buzz Lightyear's cry 'to infinity and beyond' echoes the Starship Enterprise's mission 'to boldly go where none have gone before'; the sight of toys making their way along a ventilator shaft recalls many an adventure movie — most recently *Mission Impossible* — while the troop of plastic soldiers position themselves in postures reminiscent of scenes from a hundred war films. The humour flows at two levels: that of the visual or verbal joke (Buzz Light year is referred to by a jealous Woody as 'Mr Lite Beer'); and that of the cultural observation. Rex the dinosaur sounds like a camp Woody Allen and utters such complaints as 'now I have guilt', rather in the manner of a therapy-victim. Sometimes the two levels come together, as when psychobabble meets teachers' talk in the instruction issued by Buzz to the assembled toys to 'pick a moving buddy' so that none will be left behind in the house removal.

Thus are joined the worlds of adult and of child. But they are also mixed in, and through, the films. The 'real' adults hardly appear, and the 'real' children play only walk-on parts. The main characters are kids' toys — two steps removed from adulthood. Yet the toys live adult's and not children's lives. In *Toy Story II* Potato man, catching sight of a troop of exercising Barbie dolls, resists temptation by reminding himself that he is a married man (Mrs Potato having arrived unseen at the end of the previous film).

Much cleverness has gone into the layering of ideas and images, and as will be clear to anyone who watched the documentary programme on the making of *Toy Story II*, a major source of this is the director and original story author John

Lasseter. Although familiar with the ironies and 'subverting strategies' of post-modernists, Lasseter stands in the Disney tradition of moral story-teller. But a question now arises about the meaning and value of his tales.

Lasseter's depicted world is that of suburban America with back-yards, front lawns, pet dogs, pizza parlours and the rest. Unlike the *Harry Potter* tales and similar British children's stories, there is little if any historical or literary reference. Harry, by contrast is drawn according to the archetype of the unloved fairytale orphan, friendless (and toyless). His move to a boarding school brings him companionship in a world that recalls that of Mr Chipps but also that of enchanted castles with dragons, devils and spiritual guardians. Andy faces no such comforts or threats, and those who are part of the main action — the toys — are caught up in rather ordinary capers with mundane happiness, rather than eternal gain or loss, being at stake.

The difference is traceable, I think, to the relative depth of the two cultures. Interestingly, when the first Potter tale was published in the United States it's title was changed from *Harry Potter and the Philosopher's Stone* to *Harry Potter and the Sorcerer's Stone*. That one word alteration signifies much. The 'philosopher's stone' was the substance in mediaeval mythology by which base metal could be changed into gold and was that which also bestowed eternal life. Even though British readers might be hard pressed to recall that fact of myth, nonetheless the phrase has a familiar ring for them. Not so in the US where history is often what happened earlier this decade and philosophy is generally deemed impractical and boring.

The *Toy Story* films are designed to entertain and to educate. They certainly achieve the first, but so far as the second is concerned they seem, in the terms of Woody's put-down, to offer more 'lite' than light. The crafting of moral tales is never easy, and it is no accident that the best of them draw upon stories that have evolved over many centuries and have had meaning for generation upon generation of children and adults. But, of course, the world is changing and there is less confidence in traditional norms and standards of good and bad, right and wrong. Uncertainty about one's own values is now oddly combined with confidence in the supreme importance of respecting the values of others — except, of course, when they are generally deemed to be unacceptable. Amidst this confusion it is important that film-makers go on trying to provide entertainment with a message, but we should not be too surprised if the message is nothing more than 'be nice and help one another'. These indeed are the words forever being uttered by parents and teachers, so in that sense *Toy Story* upholds tradition.

It would be a real challenge, however, for Hollywood to try to present a story for children and adults with all the depth and complexity of a traditional moral or spiritual tale. Someone might say that, unlike in the Christian era which Pope Gregory's encouragement of religious art helped shape, no such tale could now be found interesting. However, the remarkable success of the *Harry Potter* books confounds that claim. Moreover, in the person of the Warner Brothers company, American film makers set themselves precisely that challenge by choosing to make film adaptations of the Potter books. It is significant, though, that in seeking a screen writer they turned not to J.K. Rowling herself, but to Steven Cloves, author and director of *The Fabulous Baker Boys* — a knowing, and indulgently nostalgic piece of cinema that fails to find a moral lesson in the meanderings of its principal characters. Given, however, the narrative strength and determinacy of the original books and the intense commitment of readers to the unfolding tale of Harry, any screen writer and director would have had to remain close to the story lines, and be unwavering in his or her attention to the upshot of each instalment — such is the captivating power of simple moral tales.

Eleven

Making Sense of Evil

On the morning of September 11, 2001, I was sitting in the Department of Philosophy in Georgetown University in Washington DC., having taken the short route up the hill from the Potomac river. That route begins with a long flight of steep stone steps, rising up the narrow canyon between two high walls. Even if you have never been within a thousand miles of them there is a good chance that you have seen those steps, for they feature in *The Exorcist*. Often described as 'the scariest movie of all time', it is also widely regarded as one of the best films ever made.

That morning I soon learned of the attack on the Twin Towers and on the Pentagon; and with news of another plane presumed to be heading for DC the university was evacuated. I headed back down the steps, this time thinking of their associations with violent death: in the film, those of the movie director character Burke Dennings and of the exorcist, Fr Karras, both crushed by falling from on high. At the time that thought was a brief and passing one, but in the following weeks I was drawn back to it by the talk of a new confrontation with 'diabolical' evil.

In the aftermath of '9/11' it became common to speak of inhuman cruelty and wickedness. Something more than sheer violence seemed to have been unleashed upon the earth. A dark force had burst through the skin of the world. At the time, I was writing a book on the nature of religion, and in a chapter on the meaning of history drew parallels between the story of spiritual conflict related in the *Exorcist*, and the sense of a battle between good and evil expressed by both the US and its terrorist attackers.

Some while later, a copy of that book (*An Intelligent Person's Guide to Religion*) was acquired by William Peter Blatty, the author of the Oscar-winning screenplay and of the novel upon which it was based; and I later learned through a mutual acquaintance that he was intrigued by the use I had made of his theme. On the strength of this, and anticipating a return to Washington later in the year, I enquired whether Blatty might be willing to discuss his own ideas about good and evil. Initially it looked unpromising; at 77 he was hard at work on various projects and he no longer gives interviews; but in the event he was welcoming and spoke at length about his life and work. The experience was memorable.

'Bill' Blatty was born in New York to Lebanese parents who emigrated to the US on a cattle boat. His great uncle, Germanios Mouakad, was a Bishop of the Melkite Catholic church, and a leading middle-eastern philosopher. After Jesuit schooling in Brooklyn, Blatty continued to Georgetown and from there went to George Washington University to study English. He excelled throughout his studies, and in 1951 entered the Air Force, becoming chief of the policy branch of the Psychological Warfare Division.

Following a period in Beirut with the US Information Agency he moved to California and there began publishing novels. This led to script writing and by the mid-1960s he was working with Blake Edwards on a series of films, including the 1964 *Pink Panther* sequel *A Shot in the Dark*. By the end of that decade screenwriting work was drying up, so Blatty took himself off to a cabin to explore an idea that had been with him since college days. That 'exploration' issued in the novel *The Exorcist*, followed in 1973 by the legendary film.

Various accounts of the genesis and meaning of the *Exorcist* have been given. Here is what Blatty told me.

> When I was an undergraduate we were shown a number of petals that were said to have come from a miraculous fall of

flowers that occurred in 1948 in Lipa in the Phillipines. You could see on each petal an image of a woman, which because of associated apparitions was presumed to be the Virgin Mary. I noticed that my classmates were filled with a fervent desire to believe, and I accepted that if Christianity is true then nothing is as important as faith and the life of the world to come. Later, while still at Georgetown, I heard about an exorcism that had been going on partly in the area, and which was sanctioned by the Church. I thought that if this could be confirmed it would help answer questions about belief, because if there were demons then why not angels, and surely there was likely to be a God.

Years later and having little else to do I thought 'why not go back and investigate the exorcism case?'. I discovered the name of a priest involved, Fr William Bowdern. He had kept a diary of events and told me that he had no doubt it was 'the real thing'. The case involved a 14 year old boy and the episodes in question occurred in a St Louis hospital over a six week period. One inexplicable phenomenon was repeated up to thirty times a day: this was the appearance of 'branding' on the boy's body: the spontaneous occurrence of words and images. Listening to the priest and learning other details of the case, including experiences witnessed by non-religious observers, I felt that this was more than a story; it was testimony to a supernatural reality.

The book was an enormous success. 13 million copies sold in the US alone; and the movie quickly acquired a status it has never lost. Inevitably the film company wanted to make a sequel and so bought the rights. At the time, however, neither Blatty nor the director William Freedkin was interested in making a further film. The immediate sequel to the movie, *Exorcist II, The Heretic*, was not Blatty's work and it proved a flop; but he did write a follow-up novel from which he later directed a film adaptation, *Exorcist III, Legion* (1990). This starred George C. Scott as the philosophical, Jewish detective Kinderman, originally played by Lee J. Cobb. The title comes from the version in Mark's gospel of the story of Jesus casting out demons. He asks of those occupying the possessed 'what is your name?' and receives the chilling reply 'My name is Legion, for we are many'.

Blatty set one condition for our meeting—that I should have read *Legion*. I am glad I did, for it soon became clear that he is not all a 'satanic horror' writer, and is more than a weaver of terrifying tales. Behind the stories of possession and violence lies a speculative mind trying to answer two of the most ancient philosophical and theological questions: what is the source of *order* in the universe? and what is the meaning of *evil*? Blatty's debut as a director came in 1980 with *The Ninth Configuration*, another book adaptation, for which he won a Golden Globe award. The film takes its title from something quoted by one of the characters:

> In order for life to have appeared spontaneously on Earth, there first had to be hundreds of millions of protein molecules of the Ninth Configuration. But, given the size of the planet Earth, do you know how long it would take for just one of these protein molecules to appear by chance? Roughly 10 to the 243rd power, billions of years; and I find that far, far more fantastic than simply believing in a god.

A similar conclusion is arrived at by Kinderman in *Legion*, but it leads to a puzzle: '*Design and causality*, he thought. *God exists. I know*. Very nice. But what could He possibly be thinking of? Why didn't He simply intervene?'. Earlier Kinderman had reflected that 'a god who was good could not help but intervene upon hearing the cry of one suffering child. Yet he didn't. He looked on'. So, the order of the world suggests a creator God; but the evil in it seems to exclude this. What are we to think? Blatty has an answer the first part of which has familiar philosophical precedents but the second stage of which could hardly have been guessed at.

Kinderman wonders

> Was the three dimensional universe an artificial construction designed to be entered for the working out of specific problems that could be solved in no other way? Was the problem of evil in the world by design? Did the soul put on a body as men put on diving suits in order to enter the ocean and work in the depths of an alien world? Did we choose the pain that we innocently suffered?.

If there is a great good to be achieved that cannot be arrived at other than through living in a material world, and if any such world is prey to conflict as one part competes with another, then perhaps suffering is a necessary and unavoidable evil. Yet how could we possibly be said to have chosen this? After all we find ourselves born into the world without any choice in the matter, and without any purposes of our own.

So it seems. But here Blatty comes forward with an arresting idea. Suppose we *did* choose. Suppose we asked to enter the world in order to work through it to some kind of perfection. In *Legion* this idea is developed to explain the killings that occur as a result of a case of possession linked to that in the *Exorcist*. The suggestion is that we are parts or aspects of a single spirit that wanted to love the creator not out of necessity but by *choice*. And to be able to do that it/we needed to make our way through the world and back to God. But at that stage there was no material universe. There was only God and the spirit of light that we then were, whose legendary name is 'Lucifer'. The creator let us become material, and in and through that moment of becoming physical the world was made.

Discussing these ideas Bill Blatty handed me a sheaf of papers, part of the draft of a book he is working on, *Dimiter*, in which he takes his metaphysical theory further, again through the medium of a story; this one set in Albania and in Jerusalem. A character, this time a priest, explains the combination of order and suffering, of good and evil.

> 'Before the beginning,' urged the priest, in some Elsewhere, we were a single titanic being. Then something happened, some decision was made that we dimly recollect as The Fall. A means of salvation was offered. We took it. Exploding from oneness into multiplicity, we became the physical universe, space-time, light cloaked in matter, for in no other way but in bodies could we risk, could we grow and evolve back into ourself, ... Consider: all matter is finally energy. And what is energy finally? Light! ... 'You were once a bright angel.' Do you see? We are Lucifer, the 'Light Bearer,' ...

We had been talking for a few hours in Blatty's handsome study. On one wall hung photos, props, posters, and other

material charting stages and accomplishments in his career,
and beneath these stood a glowing upright juke box in classic style. On the other side of the room, beneath a light that
inexplicably and irregularly dimmed and brightened sat
my daughter Kirsty who had come along to listen to the
interview. Before leaving we moved through to a lounge
equipped with a cocktail bar on one shelf of which stood the
Exorcist Oscar. Blatty handed it to her saying 'it's a meta-
phor for Hollywood: gold plated but base metal beneath the
coating'. We were back in the familiar world of the ordinary
— as ordinary as holding an Oscar in the cocktail lounge of a
mansion in Maryland may be.

But as we made our way from the house my mind
returned to the events of September 11, to the subsequent
talk of inhuman evil, and to the usual reading of the *Exorcist*
as a film about demonic possession. If Blatty is right, then
the battle of good against evil is not one between a god in
heaven and a devil in hell, but rather is a struggle *within* the
world, between aspects of a single creature, *us*, struggling to
make its way back, of its own accord, to where it once came
from — and where it hopes to be again.

If his philosophical myth is true then there is a fallen
angel, but there are no damned demons; and unlike the
Oscar whose gilded skin conceals a body of lead, the darkness of human lives rests on a surface beneath which lies
something immeasurably good: eternal souls made out of,
and for, eternal love. Contrary to what many suppose,
Blatty's mystery tales are not horror stories but metaphysical allegories in the tradition of the ancient, near eastern cultures: stories his very ancestors might have told.

Twelve

Fiction's Enigma Variations

I have been re-reading the book of the film. So as not to spoil the story for those who have still to enjoy it, I will only mention a few features. In the opening chapter a victim is found lying sprawled on his back. He had knowledge of matters that could shake the world, and on that account had been assassinated by a member of a sinister secret society. A reluctant, but ultimately successful, amateur hero has to decipher coded information, and work out the meaning of a cryptic text. Suspected by the police of the murder, and by the secret society of having learned the truth, he is pursued by both and finds himself in Scotland.

John Buchan was a remarkable man: an outstanding student at Glasgow and Oxford; a classical scholar; a precocious editor and publisher, a gifted poet, a highly successful fiction author; a critically praised biographer and historian; a member of both Houses of Parliament; High Commissioner to the General Assembly of the Church of Scotland; and Governor General of Canada. He is also generally credited as being one of the inventors of the thriller.

In 1914 Buchan was laid up with the stomach ulcer that afflicted him all his life. Having exhausted a supply of cheap novels he decided to try his hand at writing a story of adventure and intrigue. Finished in a few weeks, it was published the following year and has remained in print ever since. The most influential thriller of all time, it is, of course, *The Thirty Nine Steps*.

The resemblance between the elements of Buchan's 'yarn' described above, and features of Dan Brown's *The Da Vinci Code* may be entirely co-incidental. Buchan's classic does not feature in Brown's announced list of favourite books and authors, though Jeffrey Archer's *Kane and Abel* is at number three, with Robert Ludlum's *Bourne Identity* series at number five. Certainly Archer and Ludlum read Buchan, and his influence, whether acknowledged or not, pervades the whole thriller genre.

The Da Vinci Code, however, establishes a new and unparalleled measure in terms of sales and impact. It is interesting, therefore, to compare the quality of these two works, the characters of the minds that produced them, and the worlds into which they were launched.

Buchan was a great storyteller and literary craftsman with a gift for describing places, even ones he had not himself seen. His classical education, brilliant mind and continuous literary activity made written language as easy for him as everyday speech. What he lacked was a capacity for characterisation. His thrillers are staffed by people drawn from a character catalogue. This is a feature shared by Brown. Indeed it might be hard to judge whether Richard Hannay or Robert Langdon is the worse drawn figure.

Hannay is a man designed to be admired by chaps: a Scot, educated by life, a colonial adventurer and mining engineer, he had acquired bush craft and had a talent for hunting. (Prof.) Langdon, by contrast, is an academic star and object of female desire: although he 'might not be considered hunk-handsome … His captivating presence is punctuated by an unusually low, baritone speaking voice, which his female students describe as "chocolate for the ears"'.

So far as stories go, Buchan occasionally strains credulity, shows deference for social position, and has a tendency to prejudice of sorts familiar in his time. Hannay reports one character's theory that: 'behind all the Governments and the armies there was a big subterranean movement engineered by very dangerous people ... educated anarchists ... financiers playing for money ... and the Jew. "Do you wonder?" he cried. "For three hundred years they have been persecuted, and this is the return match for the pogroms"'.

In 1914 mention of an international Jewish conspiracy was standard fare, but readers now recoil at the stigmatising of an ethnic or religious group as working in secret against the interests of society. Note, though, that the conspiracy is voiced by a character; for elsewhere Buchan himself praises Jews. He described Phillips Oppenheim as 'my master in fiction ... the greatest Jewish writer since Isaiah' and Buchan's name is included in the *Golden Book* of the Jewish National Fund of Israel.

Episodes in *The Code* stretch credibility even further, and there is stigmatisation a-plenty; but worse is the suggestion of scholarly research and intellectual seriousness. Having described the novel as 'drawing so heavily on the sacred feminine' Brown asserts as 'Fact' matters concerning 'The Priory of Sion' and Opus Dei. The first he describes as 'a European secret society founded in 1099—a real organisation'. The second is the group to which he attaches as a monk the 'hulking', 'limping', 'albino', self-flagellating assassin Silas.

It has been widely known for at least twenty years that 'The Priory of Sion' is a hoax created in the 20th century and that no such historical body has ever existed. The Prieuré de Sion myth was created in 1956 by a French fantasist Pierre Plantard. Meanwhile, Opus Dei is a lay organisation, not a religious order, and hence there could be no such thing as an Opus Dei monk. Turning to scriptural matters, Brown refers to the apocryphal Gospel of Philip to support the claim that Jesus was married to Mary Magdalene, and has one of his main characters, Sir Leigh Teabing, point out that in this text Mary is called 'the companion' of Jesus, and then comment that 'As any student of Aramaic will tell you, the word *companion*, in those days literally meant *spouse*'. In fact, however, the Gospel of Philip was written in Greek, not Aramaic, and the relevant Greek term, viz. *koinonós* is not generally used to mean 'spouse' but rather 'associate' or 'fellow'. Such ineptitudes, though mortifying to any serious researcher, might not matter were it not that Brown invites readers to consider (without recoil) that he is giving them an insight into a secret world of international religious conspiracy. It is perhaps unsurprising that a reviewer for the *New York Daily News* should write that 'His research is impeccable', but it is troublesome to read the *Library Journal* state that 'This masterpiece should be mandatory reading'.

Buchan's education and intelligence preserved him from intellectual pretension, and his regard for serious history established a discipline in playing with fiction. He was also a man of authentic spiritual sensibility, incapable of theological vacuity, who would have stood well clear of esoteric silliness and of slighting the faith of millions.

Perhaps the greatest difference, however, lies in the state of knowledge in the cultures into which these books were launched. In 1914 sources of ideas and historical claims were limited and tended to exist in educational contexts. There was less information but it was often filtered with an aim to promoting useful or edifying knowledge. Now, by contrast, information comes like rain, falling without regard for where it lands and often carrying pollution with it.

Fortunately, however, one quality filter remains: *the test of time*. Buchan's *Steps* are still with us nearly a century later. I doubt that Brown's *Code* will survive the decade, let alone be thrice filmed.

I am sure, nevertheless, that any further Robert Langdon esoteric cult adventures will prove enormous publishing successes. Indeed, so great has been the interest in the series that not only have there been books about the two existing books (*Angels and Demons* and the *Da Vinci Code*) there have even been books about the as-yet unwritten sequel. In spring 2006 Greg Taylor published *The Guide to Dan Brown's The Solomon Key* in which, on the basis of hints and clues, he speculates about the themes and features of a work Brown has been said to be writing. Such is the success of, and demand for the historical-sect-conspiracy genre, however, that a year later another author, Douglas Weber published a conspiracy thriller entitled *Solomon's Key: The Codis Project*.

If the speculation about Brown's sequel was accurate then Weber's book may occasion a change of title and perhaps of theme. It's all a well-kept secret, but as a coda to this discussion I am able to present what appears to be an extract from a forthcoming Dan Brown work seemingly entitled, *Elders of the Holy Rood*. I can say no more than the text came my way during a recent visit to Washington, DC, where part of the story is set. While I cannot guarantee its authenticity aspects of the layout and literary style certainly conform to those of Brown's earlier writings and the location and references correspond to elements of the anticipated *Da Vinci* sequel.

ELDERS OF THE HOLY ROOD

FACT: George Washington was initiated into Masonry in November 1752, and was elected Worshipful Master of the Old Alexandria Lodge on June 24, 1784.

The hotel described in this extract really does exist. It is situated on Seminary Drive, Alexandria, VA. It has 30 guest floors.

All descriptions of buildings, geographical locations and foodstuffs are accurate.

PROLOGUE
HILTON HOTEL, ALEXANDRIA, VIRGINIA. 8:06 A.M.

Robert Langdon stared out from the 29th floor of his hotel, across a landscape of anonymous government and company buildings set among well-groomed lawns and trees. His gaze was fixed on the pagoda-looking tower rising in the distance above the morning mist that still lay over the Potomac river.

The tower was the Masonic lodge of Old Alexandria, of which George Washington and other founding fathers had been members. It was a reminder to Langdon of the secret origins of the United States in a conspiracy of freemasons. Their aim had been to undermine the Vatican by subverting the British Empire, of which Roman Anglicanism was the established church.

Only four men knew the story, and all of them were now bones in shallow graves. Robert Langdon was more than lucky to be alive, and he knew it.

The Masonic tower was also a link back, through the *Scottish Rite*, to the country in which he and Sophie had discovered their love, and in which they had chosen to settle following the incredible *Da Vinci* adventure that had taken them to the heights and brought them to the depths.

It had been an up and down journey, but they had landed safely back in the old county in fields of shamrock and golden thistle.

Sophie remained mystically beautiful, as befitted the sole living representative of the world's most ancient royal line. Her noble features bore a striking resemblance to those of Robert Powell in Zeffirelli's *Jesus of Nazareth*.

Langdon reflected once again on just how unbelievable it was that his wife was a descendent of *Yeshua bar-Joseph* and *Miriam of Magdala*, known to history as Jesus and Mary Magdalene.

He would not have believed it himself but for his brilliance as a scholar of symbols and codes, and had there not been the obvious Powell resemblance. How remarkable a coincidence, also, that the handsome actor had been a close friend of Sophie's mother.

*   *   *

Dr. Robert Langdon was a changed man. Back then he was said by students to be 'scrumptious'. Now people looked away in embarrassment at his disfigured form. But there was still the mental brilliance. His super-rated studies had provided him with deep scholarly knowledge, as had his many hours spent exploring the internet.

He smiled knowingly as he thought of the 'Net' and the 'Web'. How ironically apt were the popular terms for a structure that had been invented by the National Security Agency to infiltrate computer systems and link them in a single super-mind working secretly on the desktops of the world.

Robert's brilliance was certainly undiminished, but his body was heavy, slow and seeping. For the last few years he had eaten little else but a confection consisting of malt nougat, topped with a layer of caramel coated in rich milk chocolate, then dipped in batter and cooked in boiling oil. He had two score of these a day, washed down with special strength heather ale.

Initially it has just been a sampling at the Roslyn fair, at which Sophie had been radiant. She had laughed teasingly '*Go on Robert, you know you have to try everything at least once*'. That had been followed by an occasional indulgence, winding down at the end of a hard slog, surfing cyberspace. But soon it was once, then twice a day, until, within a few months, he was on a dozen deep-fried chocolate bars and special ales.

Now he was up to forty of them during waking hours, with sticky patches to see him through the night. The effects had been devastating and now he was trapped in an escalating cycle of surfing and snacking.

Sophie had tried to control his habit, but his compulsions were too strong. In a desperate and remorseful effort to stop his decline she had revealed her deepest secret — the greatest secret of all human history.

Her lineage went back far further than first century Palestine. Interweaving trails of ancestry led from the eastern Mediterranean back to Scotland and forward to America. What she had told Robert about the transcontinental, subterranean cave system linking the Nile Delta, the Vale of Leven and Virginia, and about the natural channel that ran from Loch Ness to the Dead Sea, left him stunned.

Could this be the true meaning of the imagery that showed Moses with hump-like-horns, and the explanation of why, alone among all peoples, the Scots poured salt onto their oatmeal? Could it also account for the mystery of the Scottish Zionic Lodge Priory, and the three thousand year old engravings of thistles and tartan patterns found on rocks here in Alexandria? Could this be the explanation of the identical name for settlements in Scotland, Egypt and America?

Sophie had wanted to warn him of the danger of her secret, but she was too relieved that in his excitement he had set aside battered bars and ale, and seemed to have forgotten them. She could not stop him going to Virginia but hoped desperately that all would be well. After all, her secret was so deeply hidden — *how could anyone else know of it?*

* * *

Yet even now, as Robert mused at the sight of the tower, a sinister figure entered from the street into the hotel lobby and made his way to the elevator. Known only as Alex, he was a novice monk of the Scottish Executive Kirk, a secret cabal of unknown figures who had made Scotland their own fiefdom.

Alex moved slowly, limping towards his room on the 28th floor. Once there he prepared himself for what he knew he must do. Quietly he took the book from his case and settled himself on the floor to recite its terrible words. He ran his fingers in loving terror over the raised text *Standing Orders of the Scottish Parliament*. Then he began to read, rocking to and fro and banging his head on the floor. In the room below Langdon was shaken from his reverie by the sound, a steady thumping but also an unearthly and menacing chant: *grand noble rot, grand noble rot*.

What could it mean?

Then he froze as he recognised it: the words formed an uncanny anagram of his own name. He wanted to run but in his fascination he could not move.

It was true. They were all linked: the Alexandria Lodge, the Washington conspiracy, the British Imperial Vatican, the NSA, the cave system, the Dead Sea salt trail, Moses and the Zionic Priory. And as his mind span, so the chant grew louder: *grand noble rot, grand noble rot, grand noble rot …*

* * *

It was as if he had been created for this very moment. Maybe he had, maybe ... But then the ale and batter reasserted themselves in a yeasty, chocolate froth, foaming out from every pore, Robert lost consciousness. Meanwhile Alex ended his incantation, feeling relief as blood flowed freely from his bruised brow. Two good carpets were ruined, and two men's lives were about to change — forever.

* * *

Thirteen

Yarn Spinning and Soul Making

I am not sure when I first learned of the existence of the John Buchan Society, though I suspect it was in the mid 1980s and that it was as a result of one those occasional items about JB and his admirers that continue to appear in the press. At any rate at about that time, or shortly after, I became a member, and it was around then also that my wife Hilda and I were exploring in the Scottish borders and came across the John Buchan Centre in Broughton which had been opened a few years previously.

Of course my first encounter with Buchan's work came much earlier. As for many schoolboys he was my guide to a world of manly adventure in an age not felt to be appreciably different to my own. I say this to mark a contrast with Stevenson who introduced us to a past world — in which they did things differently. There is a further personal contrast in my experience of their writings. Buchan I read for myself, Stevenson was first read to me by my father, and, as I only later discovered when re-reading the likes of *Kidnapped*, he had a habit of introducing into his readings episodes and characterisations not present in the text. On more than one occasion I found myself recounting with enthusiasm an event which others clearly found it difficult to recall!

With Buchan, though, I was on my own: racing across moorland, pressing hard against the face of a cliff, slipping through a passage in St James's, looking into the eyes of a man who planned the downfall of the West, or worrying how long the thin veneer of civilisation might endure against the corrosive forces of Bolshevism, or the decadent aestheticism of fashionable London. I was also introduced to a world of society dinners where the five or ten most brilliant men of their generation were gathered, one or more of them about to embark on the adventure of their lives. The setting and form are familiar to us all, and on more than one occasion recently I found them coming to my aid.

Once was in reviewing a volume of writings by Sir Isaiah Berlin whose range and talents suggested that he was less an individual than a small population, or at any rate that he was, as Lord Rosebery said addressing Buchan, 'a multifarious man'. Born in Riga, Latvia in 1909 Berlin witnessed in Petrograd the start of the Russian revolution, and later during World War II was a political observer for the British Government in New York, Washington and Moscow. He was Chichele Professor of Social and Political Theory, the first President of Wolfson College, and a fellow of All Souls, Oxford. These besides he was President of the British Academy and a member of the Order of Merit. Berlin's achievements, his cosmopolitanism and the breadth of his interests certainly make him an honorary 'Buchaneer'.

Another occasion was when called upon to propose the toast to the honorary graduates at a University dinner. Buchan would have relished the task of celebrating the distinguished figures: a gallery director, a writer (John Le Carré, another Buchaneer), a diplomat, a lawyer, two scientists, a theologian, a philosopher and a politician. He would have looked from one to another and penned the scene. Let me remind you of the real thing, by drawing from a work to which I want to return later. Nowhere is the device of looking from one guest to another and sketching a rapid portrait of accomplishment more prominent than in Buchan's last novel *Sick Hear River*. I quote:

> Bronson Jane was almost too good to be true. He had been a noted sportsman and was still a fine polo-player; his name was a household word in Europe for his work in interna-

tional finance; he was the Admirable Crichton of his day
and it was rumoured that in the same week he had been
offered the Secretaryship of State, the Presidency of an
ancient University, and the control of a great industrial
corporation. He had chosen the third but seemed to have a
foot in every other world.

Of another guest we learn

He is on the Johns Hopkins staff and is making a big name
for himself in lung surgery ... He had a pretty good training
—Harvard—two years at Oxford—a year in Paris—a long
spell in a Montreal hospital.

Of another

His father left him all kinds of wealth, but Walter wasted no
time in getting out of oil into icebergs. He has flown and
mushed and tramped over most of the Arctic, and there are
heaps of mountains and wild beasts named after him.

And of yet another

His line is deep learning. He's about our foremost pundit -
professor at Yale—dug up cities in Asia Minor—edited
Greek books. Writes very nice little stories too. That's
Clifford Savery.

Buchan's *Free Fishers*. is another classic 'yarn' of the type
of which he was one of the creators. As in *The 39 Steps*, a
clean limbed and wholesome hero finds himself at odds
with one of the most dangerous men in the country and has
to combat time, space and villainy in order to reach a destination before a decent chap is killed. In this case, however,
the hero is not the uncerebral Richard Hannay but the scholarly young Professor of Logic and Rhetoric in the University of St Andrews, Mr Anthony Lammas. The novel starts
at night with Lammas hurrying back along the cliff tops to
St Andrews. As he reflects on his condition our narrator
takes up the story:

His classes were popular and orderly, and many consulted
him on private concerns which they would not have
broached to any other professor. Also to salve his con-
science, he began to cultivate a special gravity in his
deportment.... Yet all the while he was nursing his private
fire of romance in the manuscripts accumulating in his

study drawers, and once in a while those fires were permitted to flicker in public.

Rightly bored in Senate, a scourge of colleagues purloining books from the College library, a great debater with Dr Witherspoon the Professor of Moral Philosophy, Mr Andrew Lammas is, like all of Buchan's heroes, a great success. Indeed, Buchan has been criticised for his cult of achievement. This is not the time or place to defend him but we must understand that he had himself been astonishingly successful in several departments of life and he respected accomplishment in others. Regarding it in part, I suspect, as a Calvinist form of penance. In fact it might be said of JB that in general he had a greater feeling for ideas than for motivations. Was he himself, then a philosopher?

In *Memory Hold-the-Door* Buchan tells us that he 'came to philosophy quite naturally as a consequence of [his] youthful theological environment', and goes on to relate how he first read in the subject before taking classes in philosophy at Glasgow University and continued to read avidly, so that by the time he went to Oxford he had done most of the reading required for the final examinations. He confesses, however, that while he maintained his interest beyond university, shortly before the Great War his attention shifted from philosophy to history. Subsequently he remarks, with self-insight; 'Had I been a professed philosopher I should have been forced to crystallise my thought, but, as it was, I could afford to keep it, so to speak, in solution'.

Certainly JB was not an academic philosopher, and nor do I think that he could have been comfortable with the fine detail of epistemology, metaphysics or moral theory. At the same time, however, he clearly had a romantic liking for the vast mysteries of the universe. In one short story 'Space' (first published in *Blackwood's Magazine* in 1911 and reprinted in *The Moon Endureth*) metaphysical speculations about the nature of space and time are explored.

The epigraph to the tale is a version of Tertullian's famous paradox concerning the Christian faith '*Est impossibile?*

Certum est' (it is impossible? it is certain); and reference is made to (invented) articles in *Mind* (then, as now, the main British philosophy journal). The narrator describes being told a strange story by Sir Edward Leithen — to whom I shall return shortly.

> 'Odd that you didn't know Hollond. You must have heard his name. I thought you amused yourself with metaphysics.'
>
> Then I remembered. There had been an erratic genius who had written some articles in *Mind* on that dreary subject, the mathematical conception of infinity. Men had praised them to me, but I confess I never quite understood their argument.

It turns out that Hollond had a theory about the mathematical structure of space and that he had begun to enter mentally into this structure, 'a world of pure reason'.

Although the articles, like their author Hollond, were fictional, I suspect they may have been borrowed from fact. Buchan knew and was encouraged, as a barrister and as an aspiring politician, by R.B. Haldane, a fellow-Scot, a philosopher-politician and later Lord Chancellor. In 1907 Haldane gave as his Presidential Address to the Aristotelian Society 'The Methods of Modern Logic and the Conception of Infinity', in which he writes 'nature is not prior in time to mind, but arises in and through its distinctions'. There is in this the foundation of a kind of metaphysical idealism.

Hollond's subsequent experiences and his death move us, however, from metaphysics to mysticism. In this connection I think it is very important to take note of Buchan's sense of the occult. I once planned to write (and *Deo volente* I may yet do so) an essay to be entitled 'Buchan's Mystical Thrills'. The subject of this would be the idea, recurrent in his writings, of our living on the edge of one world; with another, better known to our ancestors, lying not far beyond. That other world is not obviously the supernatural domain as this is envisaged by the Christian, i.e. a world ordained by Grace— though it may be its complement, namely a world ruled by dangerous spirits.

There is another sense, however, in which Buchan was drawn to philosophy where this is to be understood in accord with its etymology, *viz.* as love of wisdom *philosophia*. This indeed was the understanding of the Greeks and Romans whose writings he studied and from which he continued to take inspiration. Earlier I mentioned *Sick Heart River*. This was Buchan's last work. His biographer Janet Adam Smith has observed that in this 'he transcends the limit of the adventure story and writes his own testament'. In contrast to the unintrospective memoir *Memory Hold the Door*, *Sick Heart River* is, I believe, a work of broadly philosophical self-examination conducted through the character of Sir Edward Leithen. Buchan was ill. Leithen is told he is dying. Buchan had come to know the Canadian north through his occupancy of the Governor-Generalship. Leithen goes there in search of a man lost. Both men were in the process of making their souls; taking stock and coming to terms with death. *Sick Heart River* was begun in 1939 and Buchan passed away in 1940 a few weeks before the date set in the novel for the death of Sir Edward. The work is moving and wise, and a few years ago I was pleased to have the opportunity to pass a copy of the American edition (*Mountain Meadow*) to the then Governor-General of Australia Sir Ninian Stephen who, unsurprisingly, was already a Buchan admirer.

The phrase 'making one's soul' I take from a little known address delivered by Buchan at Birkbeck College, London. He writes

> In old days people had a phrase about a man's 'making his soul'. You retired from politics or business or soldiering, or whatever was your profession, and went into retreat, before you died, in order to possess your soul, to settle accounts with life, and make your peace with heaven. We do not talk like that today, and yet the duty is still imperative; the only difference is that we now realise that such a thing is not to be done only in seclusion in the twilight of life. It is a process that should be going on all your days … It

is only when we see a thing in its proper perspective in the scheme of the world that we find it easy to renounce and pass on.

This is philosophical wisdom of an ancient sort familiar from the stoics and Christian writers in the tradition that urges detachment or abandonment. It also casts *Sick Heart River* in a light of spiritual reflection. But, of course, it is not a philosophy of total disengagement. Buchan knew that the practical business of life had to go on and that moral, philosophical and spiritual values have a necessary role in shaping society and politics as well as the soul. He was in that respect a resoundingly practical figure. In his little study of Aquinas, Chesterton writes that since the modern world began no-one's philosophy has corresponded to everyone's sense of reality. That is an achievement Buchan would have admired: as he once said in a House of Commons' debate: 'Personally I would rather take the view of a Border shepherd on most questions than of all the professors of Europe'.

Fourteen

Taking Thought
Seriously

Some viewers of BBC 1's *Question Time*, chaired by David
Dimbleby, may be unaware that it is a television adaptation
of the long-running radio programme *Any Questions* (presented by his brother Jonathan). The latter began in 1948 in
the West Country but went national in 1950. The following
year Anthony Wedgwood Benn appeared on the team and
has since made over 80 further appearances, more than any
other contributor.

Like *Desert Island Discs*, and the *Archers* (indeed like Tony
Benn), *Any Questions* is a national institution; but, like these
others also, it has changed to reflect the style and manners
of the times. In the early days it was not permitted to discuss
any matter that had been before Parliament in the previous
two weeks. Now it often starts with a question about that
day's events at Westminster.

It also shared something of the cerebral character of
another panel discussion *The Brains Trust*. This began in
1942 and by the end of the war had a regular audience of
almost a third of the UK population. It too spawned a television version broadcast in the 1950s, and was later reprised
for radio under the chairmanship of Joan Bakewell.

Such broadcasting was unapologetically intelligent, even
intellectual. It often drew from academia and the worlds of
letters and of science, and presumed an educated audience
that did not expect to understand everything that might be

said, but which would take its ignorance as something to be aware of and, if opportunity permitted, to be remedied. That, after all, was a point of such programmes.

Any Questions swam in the same waters, though properly it was more topical. Today it continues to engage matters of the moment but tends to be primarily political and controversialist. These are not ignoble ends, but there is a danger that having entered the shallows of current combat, the depths of perennial problems are avoided as too cold and deep, and insufficiently entertaining.

A recent programme, however, offered a glimpse into those depths in the form of a reply to a question in the 'lighter' category that usually appears towards the end. An audience member asked 'Which of your teachers and lecturers had the most impact on you and why?'.

Ben Bradshaw (*Labour*) spoke of an inspiring History master and an eccentric German teacher, and was responded to, so the BBC transcript shows, with '[CLAPPING]'. Oliver Walston (*Farming interest*) spoke of a house-master who was a bad teacher 'so he hasn't taught me anything, and didn't inspire me to great works of literature. But he got me off my bum and that was quite an achievement.' [LAUGHTER]'. Kat Fletcher (*National Union of Students*) identified an environment rather than a person, describing the benefits to a 16 year old school leaver of going into a local further education college. The transcript does not record any audience reaction to this reply.

Finally, Oliver Letwin (*Conservative*) spoke of two 'great university teachers': the eminent political historian Maurice Cowling (recorded by the BBC as 'Morris') and

> greatest of the teachers I had, a lady [philosopher] called Professor Elizabeth Anscombe, who … would go from one end of the board to the other and put up things under the heading 'murder' or 'killing'. And various things after about 20 minutes would be rubbed out and put on the other side of the board. This was entirely mysterious for some months … eventually I managed to penetrate what she was talking about, and it completely transformed my understanding of human intentionality. And she made me realise

what it is actually to think about something in a really sustained way. And I don't think you can do that actually in any way than through that process'.

At this point farmer Walston asked 'what the word human intentionality meant' [LAUGHTER] and Letwin's self-deprecating reply suggested he was embarrassed at having perhaps misjudged the occasion by speaking seriously and in highbrow terms.

Letwin had the immense privilege of having been taught 'up close and personal', as the BBC might now say, by the most brilliant of Wittgenstein's students. Anscombe is widely regarded as one of the best philosophers of the twentieth century. It sometimes took readers years to see the point of what she was arguing, but this was because she always took on the hardest problems and had no time for slick presentation. She is reported to have said to A.J. Ayer 'if you didn't talk so quickly, people wouldn't think you were so clever' — though, in fairness his reply should also be quoted: 'if you didn't talk so slowly, people wouldn't think you were so profound.'

From her student days she had discussed and written about issues of moral, political and religious interests. In 1939, as a student, she co-authored a pamphlet predicting that Britain's conduct in World War II would be unjust, and in 1956/7 she protested the award by the University of Oxford of an honorary degree to President Truman, charging that he had commanded the murderous use of nuclear weapons against innocent Japanese civilians.

In her anthology *Women Philosophers* (1996), Mary Warnock describes Anscombe as 'the undoubted giant among women philosophers'. She certainly has a good claim to be the greatest woman philosopher of history.

In the past, such distinction would have merited a BBC profile. Following her death in 2001 *Woman's Hour* carried an item on her and Melvyn Bragg's *In Our Time* has the standing and intellectual ambition to take on such a subject. But for now we only have the embarrassed laughter of *Any Questions*, and the contrast between Letwin talking seriously for a minute or two, and his leader David Cameron laying out his treasures on *Desert Island Discs*. Musically he will be comforted and inspired by Bob Dylan, Benny Hill, Pink Floyd, Kiri Te Kanawa, Radiohead, the Smiths, R.E.M, and The Killers' 'All these Things that I've Done'. And for the written word he has *The River Cottage Cookbook* by Hugh Fearnley-Whittingstall. As Anscombe might have said, there is not much to think about here.

Who was Elizabeth Anscombe? where and when did she live? and what was her philosophy? Although she was unquestionably brilliant and wrote on a wide range of topics including ethical and religious issues, Anscombe is not widely known outside academic philosophy. In this respect she differs from continental figures such Hannah Arendt (1906–75) or Simone De Beauvoir (1908–86); and from British philosophers such as her contemporaries Iris Murdoch (1919–99), Mary Midgley (1919–), and Mary Warnock (1924–).

There are several reasons for her relative obscurity. Anscombe moved in the depths of thought, and when she surfaced, her utterances often seemed puzzling and hard to comprehend; or else startling, uncompromising and counter to prevailing orthodoxies. Relatedly, she hated superficiality and trendiness and took a low view of the values of contemporary society. Also, while she was capable of great kindness and generosity, she could be ferocious and scathing in criticism.

Her impact on the culture of ideas should be judged not by immediate fame and influence but by its cumulative effect over decades. Increasingly, she will come to be seen not only as the finest woman philosopher of the twentieth century, but as something of a prophetic figure who saw in her own times the shape of the future.

Elizabeth Anscombe was born in Limerick in 1919. Her father had been posted to Ireland as a British army officer but later the family returned to England where he resumed teaching at Dulwich College. In 1937 Anscombe went up to Oxford, and although neglecting ancient history in favour of philosophy she still came away with a brilliant First Class degree. Following research in Oxford and Cambridge, she was awarded a position at Somerville, Oxford where she remained until her appointment in 1970 as Professor of Philosophy in Cambridge.

Several important events occurred during her student years. Through teenage reading, Anscombe had discovered Catholicism and in 1938 joined the Church. Interestingly, two other strong-minded women philosophers, and near contemporaries, (St) Edith Stein (1891–1942) and Simone Weil (1909–43) had also found themselves drawn in that direction, though Anscombe would not, I think, have known of either of them. In the same year, however, she met another philosopher convert, Peter Geach, whom she married in 1941 and they later had seven children.

In 1939, along with another student (Norman Daniels) she wrote, published and distributed *The Justice of the Present War Examined* in which she argued that the war would lead to aerial bombing of German cities and the killing of civilians. This was to be the beginning of a life-long commitment to denouncing what she saw as institutionalised murder.

After the war she got to know Wittgenstein who came to regard her as the best of his students, and entrusted to her the task of translating his work. He also appointed her one of his literary executors and, although distanced from the Catholicism of his childhood, in his final months he asked that she put him in touch with 'a non-philosophical priest'. She introduced him to Fr Conrad Pepler, the Dominican who had received her into the Church, and Pepler later conducted Wittgenstein's funeral. Fifty years on in 2001, Dominicans oversaw her own funeral and interment in a Cambridge grave close by that of her teacher and friend.

Anscombe's narrowly academic writings concern logic, language, metaphysics, mind, and action, and the relation of the last of these to questions in ethics. In 1957 she gave a radio talk entitled 'Does Oxford Moral Philosophy Corrupt Youth?'. It is heavily ironic, arguing that to be corrupted by Oxford teaching you would otherwise have to have fared better, but such was the general culture that youth is corrupted anyhow. She concluded 'This [Oxford] philosophy is conceived perfectly in the spirit of the time and might be called the philosophy of the flattery of that spirit'.

The immediate effect was outrage, with a fiery correspondence in the BBC magazine the *Listener* that deserves to be dramatised. In the course of replying to one philosopher critic, Anscombe cites the view that using nuclear weapons against the Japanese was justified by the balance of effects, and replying to another she introduces the term 'consequentialist' to describe someone who says what is right is what has the best overall consequences. In those days a revolution was begun in moral philosophy.

Shortly beforehand, Anscombe had again published a pamphlet, this time arguing that President's Truman's decision to order nuclear attacks on Hiroshima and Nagasaki was murderous, and protesting Oxford University's decision to award him an honorary degree. Her motion to oppose this only had the support of *three* others, one being her colleague the philosopher Philippa Foot.

Anscombe concluded that by saying that all Truman had done was sign an order with good consequences in view, her opponents showed that they did not understand either action or morality. A flood of brilliant publications followed of which the most comprehensive is an essay 'Modern Moral Philosophy' whose meaning and implications are still being debated half a century later.

As a correlative to insisting on moral responsibility Anscombe argued devastatingly against the belief in determinism. And having addressed the metaphysics of freedom she returned to the issue of how human dignity should be respected in our practices and policies. In the 1950s she predicted that a society willing to bomb civilians would have no difficulty institutionalising abortion and euthanasia. Seeing us acclimatising to the destruction of helpless life she took her protests from the seminar to the street and late in life was arrested and carried off for protesting outside an abortion clinic. She always practised her philosophy.

Fifteen

Making Sense of Religion

The concept or, if one prefers, the 'phenomenon' of religion is evidently somewhat indeterminate. It has clear instances: Judaism, Christianity, Islam, Hinduism, and so on; but, and this is why 'and so on' is not that helpful, there are less clear cases, such as Taoism, and progressively more doubtful ones, e.g. falun-gong, the Aquarian foundation, and scientology.

The web site 'Adherents.com' lists over 4,000 'religions, churches, denominations, religious bodies, faith groups, tribes, cultures, movements, ultimate concerns, etc' — notice again the terminal drift into vagueness marked by 'etc'. Even restricting oneself to more or less clear cases, however, there are vast numbers of religious believers throughout the world. Indeed, of the six and a half billion humans on the globe about 80% belong to recognised religions, about 33% are Christians, holding allegiance to teachings only formulated quite recently in the history of human kind, and half of the latter are Roman Catholics. Arguably nothing compares with religion as a domain of commitment, and no other extensive commitment so unifies humanity, even when it divides it. What then explains the origins of religion and its power to have and to hold the allegiance of so many?

One answer is that religion gives expression to a universal need to acknowledge and respond to a sense of cosmic order and human 'creatureliness'. In writing that 'ever since the creation of the world [God's] invisible nature, namely his eternal power and deity, has been clearly perceived in the things that have been made' (*Romans*), St Paul was expressing an idea familiar to him prior to his conversion. A century beforehand, Cicero wrote 'what can be so obvious and clear, as we gaze up at the sky and observe the heavenly bodies, as that there is some divine power of surpassing intelligence by which they are ordered' (*On the Nature of the Gods*). Four centuries earlier, Empedocles observed that matter is inanimate and hence must be moved by another, from which he concluded that ultimately there must be some intrinsic principles of attraction and repulsion — which he termed 'Love' and 'Strive'. Earlier still and in other cultures the idea of a transcendent source of existence, order and movement seems to have been prevalent, a reflective response to experience.

Another possibility is that religion originates in an innate idea. Experiences of wonder may elicit it, but it is not a conclusion derived from them; rather we have inbuilt within us a notion of a supreme other, and an attitude of awe or piety towards the world as the work of that 'Other'. Initially the idea might be embryonic and ill-defined, but given time it could grow into natural religion. And the god(ish) idea might, as St Anselm and Descartes supposed, have been put there by God Himself — in order that we should have a good chance of coming to know and to love Him.

A third answer might be developed by drawing on something else that Empedocles is reported to have said, namely, that whenever things turned out as they would have done if they were happening for a purpose then creatures survived, but when this did not happen they perished. Suppose, then, that religion does indeed derive from an idea in our minds but that this idea has not been arrived at by our observing nature or ourselves, or been put there for a purpose, but instead is simply the result of an ancient accident of circumstance which has survived because it brings certain advantages. Suppose in other words that religion is a product of blind evolution.

Since the thinkers of classical antiquity had the intellectual resources to advance this suggestion one might wonder why they did not favour it. The answer may be that they realised that it is a bad explanation because it fails to address the nature of religious beliefs as *beliefs*. What needs to be accounted for is why people actually hold to certain ideas and engage in particular practices, and part of that explanation will involve their *beliefs* about the point and value of those religious notions and practices. The fact that ancestors behaving in related ways thereby enjoyed certain reproductive benefits, hardly touches the issue. Or so one might think.

Herein, however, enters a striking advocate of evolutionism: a highly talented, highly voluble professor of mind, reason and science, determined to expose religion as a product of purely natural and entirely unpurposeful forces; and then to suggest that whatever benefits its distant relatives might once have conferred, the phenomenon as *we* have it is best dispensed with—and the sooner the better, for it is a cause of needless misery.

Daniel Dennett has been a significant presence on the philosophical scene since the publication of his first book (*Content and Consciousness*) in 1969; and in the intervening years he has developed highly distinctive lines of thought about the nature of mind and consciousness. Given the subtlety of his work any brief characterisation risks oversimplification, so let me just leap in with a two word summary: Dennett is an *iconoclastic demytholigiser*. Let any of the great themes of metaphysics and religion pass before his gaze: consciousness, rationality, free-will, the soul, God, and he will be at them tearing away until no vestige of the metaphysical remains: for Dennett, all that there (really) is, is matter in motion—though as he would no doubt say, that is no small show.

Materialism can be maintained as a quiet intellectual conviction, shared among like-minded scholars, but Dennett is an evangelist, and having recognised what he believes to be the truth he wants to shout it in the highways and byways, and will not rest content until no-one will be able to persist in their error with the excuse that they have not heard the good news.

And the gospel is as follows:[1]

1) 'religions are *social systems whose participants avow belief in a supernatural agent or agents whose approval is to be sought'* (p. 9);

2) 'religion is a human phenomenon composed of events, organisms, objects, structures, patterns and the like that all obey the laws of physics or biology, and hence do not involve miracles' (p. 25);

3) 'if we want to know why we value the things we love, we need to delve into the evolutionary history of the planet, uncovering the forces and constraints that have generated the glorious array of things we treasure. Religion is not exempt from this' (p. 53);

4) 'religion is a human phenomenon, it is a hugely costly endeavour, and evolutionary biology shows that nothing so costly just happens ... the ultimate measure of evolutionary 'value' is *fitness*, the capacity to replicate more successfully than the competition' (p. 69);

5) 'cultural transmission can *sometimes* mimic genetic transmission, permitting competing variants to be copied at different rates, resulting in gradual revisions [that] *have no deliberate foresighted authors'* (p. 78);

6) 'We can tentatively work backward, extrapolating under the guidance of our fundamental biological constraint: each innovative step had to "pay for itself" somehow, in the *existing* environment in which it first occurred, independently of whatever its role might become in later environments' (p. 102);

7) 'The memorable nymphs and fairies and goblins and demons that crowd the mythologies of every people are the imaginative offspring of a hyperactive habit of finding agency wherever anything puzzles or frightens us. ... The [myths] that get shared and remembered are

[1]   Quotations from *Breaking the Spell: Religion as a Natural Phenomenon*, Daniel C. Dennett (Allen Lane/Penguin 2006).

the souped-up winners of billions of competitions for rehearsal time in the brains of our ancestors' (p. 123-4);

8) 'Innate curiosity, stimulated by music and rhythmic dancing and other forms of 'sensory pageantry' could probably account for the initial motivation to join the chorus' (p. 148);

9) '[religion] is a finely attuned amalgam of brilliant plays and stratagems, capable of holding people enthralled and loyal for their entire lives' (p. 154);

10) 'free-floating rationales that are blindly sculpted by earlier competitions can come to be augmented or even replaced by *represented* rationales ... [ones that are] *used* — argued over, reasoned about, agreed upon (p. 177).

Having developed this series of steps, Dennett then moves to consider two questions: first, whether folk religions, and the organized religions they have become, have conferred fitness benefits on their practitioners; and second, whether, religions are morally deserving of allegiance and service. Since the announced purpose of the book is to 'break the spell' of religion, which has hitherto protected it from serious scientific analysis and critical evaluation, and to expose it to empirical testing, Dennett makes a point of saying that the answers to these questions now remain to be determined. But that unassuming nicety observed, it is pretty clear that he has come to a conclusion and that he feels that open-minded readers will share it: good motives and occasional benefits allowed for, religion is a bad thing, and the good sometimes associated with it could be got otherwise.

The book is a brick (450 pages) possibly suitable for breaking church windows — but was it designed as such? In dealing with artifacts one needs to distinguish between intended purposes and incidental effects. I assume that Dennett intended his book to be read not thrown; but it can be thrown and its use as a missile might confer reproductive benefits on those who so deploy it. The logic of evolutionary explanations requires, however, that one discriminate between heritable adaptations that have been selected for *per se* because of the advantages they confer, and incidental by-products selected *per accidens*. It may have been the case that objects of the rough size, shape and weight of Dennett's book were used by his ancestors and are used by his contemporaries as missiles. but that doesn't settle the question of the actual point of the book. Is its being a book, or a potential weapon, an intended or incidental feature of its manufacture? I shall assume that the answer is clear.

Likewise with religion. Whatever benefits may have attached, or do attach, to engaging in certain forms of behaviour, the question we need to address in understanding religion is the meaning and value of that behaviour, and its associated beliefs and values, *as religious expressions*, not as evolutionary adaptations. Readers should already have a sense that there is (as there must be) a great deal of pure conjecture in Dennett's speculations about our ancestral past, but even when they make for interesting reading they are beside the point so far as concerns the obvious issues raised by religious claims, viz. what do they mean and are they true?

Dennett is too bright simply to have missed this, but he is driven by the conviction that religious claims are not true, and are even of dubious coherence; therefore, confronted by the fact that they are so widely voiced, he assumes that they must have some other kind of explanation. Consider by analogy the situation of an adult who reports each morning that a golden fairy visited her in the night and told her stories about the building of a fairy queen's silken castle. To engage in discussion with the woman about the details of the conversations would be at most a calming move preparatory to seeking a clinical diagnosis. Most people would not even consider the possibility that the narrative was factual — and anyone who did would themselves be subject to the presumption of disorder.

Dennett does consider whether religious beliefs might be true, but the brevity, barely six pages, and the dismissive character of the discussion speak volumes. The stuff of supernaturalism is to him no more credible than that of fairyism, indeed it is probably less so since he might observe that unlike fairyism, Godism is not experimentally testable. This is not the occasion to respond, yet it is important to assure readers who may feel the weight of Dennett's prose weighing down upon them that the pressure is eminently resistable. Often witty, sometimes jovial, and occasionally tender, Dennett is also somewhat domineering, hardly allowing the reader pause to take breath or to develop responses.

He writes in the preface that the book is addressed primarily to American readers 'the curious and conscientious citizens of my native land — as many as possible, not just the academics'. Later he writes of 'religious folk' as if speaking to members of a suburban congregation; but he can't really imagine that the folk will read this, or that if philosophically-trained believers do so that they will be unsettled by it. My guess is that the intended purpose of the book is to say a lot out loud, with the hoped for incidental effect that others might listen. In truth, however, this is a personal testament unlikely to win many converts.

So we end where we began with the fact of billions of believers and with the ancient suggestion that religion is a natural response to the universal sense of being in a world created and governed, by what and to what end one does not quite know. Whether that sense of creation and creatureliness is warranted is indeed a question for investigation, but it calls for attention to the content of religious claims and requires some assessment of their plausibility. The spell of religion is the sense that those claims, however problematic, register something of the truth about the nature of human beings and their place in the cosmos. However evolution proceeds, so long as humans continue to experience and reflect, then religion will remain a pervasive aspect of their existence.

Sixteen

Arguing Over God

Recently the debate about the existence of God and the nature of religion has intensified, with believers and atheists arguing forcefully on both sides of the divide. While people of faith say with renewed vigour that the universe is the product of a benign deity, and that religion is a mode of spiritual response through which creatures may approach their Creator, atheists match their conviction with their view that there is no God and that religion is deceptive mythology. But as well as the passion there is also mounting rancour as some of those on both sides have begun to accuse their opponents of stupidity or malevolence.

Twenty years ago the intellectual lead was with the theists. They were inspired by a number of able mainstream philosophers who had applied themselves to issues in natural theology (pre-eminently Richard Swinburne in Britain and Alvin Plantinga in the United States), and by a cluster of distinguished scientists (including John Polkinghorne in Britain and Frank Tipler in the US) who saw evidence for theism in the structure of the physical world, and in our ability to comprehend it.

After a long period sheltering underground, intellectual theism was again striding out with confidence. With books and articles appearing, publishers and broadcasters got the sense of a trend and encouraged head-to-head encounters between believers and unbelievers. One product of this was a published debate between the prominent Australian atheist philosopher J.J.C. Smart and myself, which appeared under the title *Atheism and Theism*, first in 1996 and then in a second edition in 2003. It was widely reviewed and generated a secondary literature enlarging the areas of dispute.

In the last few years it has been the atheists who have been most vocal, publishing books for the educated public. Americans Sam Harris and Daniel Dennett (see chap. 15), and Britons Richard Dawkins and Christopher Hitchens, have launched vehement attacks on religion, rejecting the view that it is reasonable and benign and instead accusing it of being a refuge of the unthinking and the malevolent, and that those who argue for it are either knaves or fools.

If that were not souring enough, matters have just taken a definite turn for the worse. On Sunday 4 November 2007, *The New York Times Magazine* published a lengthy article entitled 'The Turning of an Atheist'. The author, Mark Oppenheimer, is a freelance journalist and sometime editor who has written before on the place of religion in America. Within a couple of weeks, however, this article had already become his best-known work. For in it he drew from and entered into the world of internet religious polemics, touching the charged issue of whether or not one of the best-known philosophical atheists had turned from nothingness to God.

The philosopher in question is Antony Flew and the story Oppenheimer tells is one of suggested exploitation and misrepresentation, with theists and atheists pulling an elderly and failing man hither and thither to advance their own interests—Flew was 84 at the time of the article's publication.

Of necessity Oppenheimer has to speculate, and evidently he is not an altogether neutral commentator. At one point he writes, 'Depending on whom you ask, Antony Flew is either a true convert whose lifelong intellectual searchings finally brought him to God or a senescent scholar possibly being exploited by his associates.' It is clear that he favours the second suggestion. Whatever the true answer, however, there are points in the Flew affair that should give anyone involved in debating God and religion cause to pause and to consider how far one should be willing to go in pursuing and campaigning for one's convictions.

As it happens I have a privileged perspective on one aspect of the affair, for I am a character in the story. In 2004, an American businessman and amateur philosopher named Roy Abraham Varghese convened a meeting at New York University between Antony Flew, an Israeli physicist Gerald Schroeder, and myself for the purpose of producing a documentary film of an extended encounter and discussion on the subject of the existence of God. Varghese, an Indian Syro-Malankara-rite Catholic, had a long-standing interest in natural theology and was evidently very well read in, and comprehending of, analytical philosophy of religion. Indeed the previous year he had published a book, *The Wonder of the World*, in which he drew upon this and scientific literature to present an extended argument for the reality of God. Varghese was also familiar with Flew, having had dealings with him for 20 years. He had previously brought him to the US for seminars and conferences.

I was invited to the 2004 event on the strength of my previous debate with Smart. When I accepted the invitation I imagined that we would be on a panel before an audience of academics and interested members of the public (as had been the case with Smart in Melbourne in 2000). So the setting of a television studio without audience or director proved challenging, in no small part because we were placed for long periods beneath intense studio lights. Still, we did our best with unscripted pieces to camera, and two- and three-way discussion.

What was notable was that in the course of this, Flew, who had long been regarded as one of the leading philosophical atheists, yielded to arguments favouring the existence of God and also to ones defending this hypothesis against the counter-argument from the facts of natural and moral evil.

The following description by Oppenheimer of the film of these discussions gives a sense of the events, and of his take on them:

> When at last Flew speaks, his diction is halting, in stark contrast to Schroeder and Haldane, both younger men,

forceful and assured. Under their prodding, Flew concedes that the Big Bang could be described in Genesis; that the complexity of DNA strongly points to an 'intelligence'; and that the existence of evil is not an insurmountable problem for the existence of God. In short, Flew retracts decades' worth of conclusions on which he built his career. At one point, Haldane is noticeably smiling, embarrassed (or pleased) by Flew's acquiesence. After one brief lecture from Schroeder, arguing that the origin of life can be seen as a form of revelation, Flew says, 'I don't see any way to meet that argument at the moment.'

Our meeting was entirely congenial, and Flew and I talked agreeably before, during and after the filming. I knew him from previous occasions in the US and in the UK, and it is of little surprise, therefore, that I might be seen to be smiling. It is also true that I was pleased that Flew conceded cogency to my case for God and to my response to the problem of evil.

It is interesting, and perceptive, however, that Oppenheimer suggests that I might have shown some embarrassment, since I did not think that Flew's acquiescence was demanded by the force of the points. Replies might have been mounted, which I would have expected, and to which I would then have responded. But in the event I sensed that the exchange was unlikely to go to further rounds and registered that his vigour was reduced. Thereafter my engagement with him was more in the manner of an interview than a debate.

On our return to the UK, I wrote, as I had promised, to send him the relevant sections from my earlier exchange with Smart; and Flew in turn sent me an introduction he had written to a reprint of his well-known book *God and Philosophy*, in which he set out his new attitude to the arguments in favour of the existence of God.

So far as I was concerned that was the end of things. But shortly after, the fires began to burn. Varghese had produced an edited, illustrated, soundtracked and commentary-accompanied DVD of the New York discussions under the title *Has Science Discovered God?* and begun marketing this as providing a record of Flew's departure from atheism.

Associated Press and other agencies picked up the story and very soon the internet was aflame with praise or denunciation. Atheist groups sought to defuse the significance of the reports, suggesting that they were confused or even deceitful; or else proposing that if accurate they were to be explained by Flew's mental decline. Theists meanwhile sang praises and thanksgiving for the return of a lost soul and began to heap glories upon him. In 2006 Biola, an Evangelical Christian university in California, awarded Flew the Phillip E. Johnson Award for Liberty and Truth, named after the author of *Darwin on Trial*, a sustained attack on the materialist assumptions of evolutionary naturalism.

These responses are as nothing when compared to the predictable reactions to a book published late in 2007 entitled *There is a God: How the World's Most Notorious Atheist Changed his Mind*, described as being 'by Antony Flew with Roy Abraham Varghese'. I quote the form of the authorial assignment for it is part of Oppenheimer's suggestion that Flew had little if anything to do with the book and that it is the latest and most brazen attempt by a member of the theist forces to co-opt a declining mind to their cause.

A couple of week's after Oppenheimer's article Roy Varghese published a letter in *The New York Times Magazine* rejecting the suggestion of misrepresentation, and the publisher, Harper, was reported to have put out a statement on Flew's behalf in which he is quoted as saying: 'My name is on the book and it represents exactly my opinions. I would not have a book issued in my name that I do not 100 per cent agree with. I needed someone to do the actual writing because I'm 84 and that was Roy Varghese's role. The idea that someone manipulated me because I'm old is exactly wrong. I may be old but it is hard to manipulate me. This is my book and it represents my thinking.'

As with the defences and denunciations on the weblogs, readers will interpret these statements and Oppenheimer's article in line with their own prejudices, but to my mind the presumption should be in favour of innocence. That said, I felt uneasy about what I read regarding the 2004 event. This includes misleading descriptions of Flew's position, which I took to be that while there is evidence in nature of intelligent creation, there is also evidence to suggest that who or whatever created the world is not concerned with the welfare of its creatures.

This is certainly not theism, and in one understanding of the term, as Flew himself has pointed out, it could even be described as a form of a-theism. Certainly I had, and still have, no reason to think that Flew has embraced theism; and nor have I had any reason to think that he regards Christianity as at all plausible. Indeed its doctrine of a loving creator God is one that he took to be at odds with what we know about the cosmos. Where his thinking led him subsequently I do not know. Flew and I have not corresponded since the period immediately following the New York meeting. Nor have I been involved in any discussions about influencing his views, and nor had I commented publicly on them prior to the publication of Oppenheimer's article.

The arguments and controversies surrounding Flew's announced abandonment of atheism are a reflection of the state of religious and anti-religious polemics in the US. Until now the issue of Flew's changing views about atheism has received little commentary in Britain but that may be changing. If so it will be further evidence of the vulgarisation of intellectual debate, for what matters is not the prejudices of the parties but the truth or falsity of the God hypothesis and the cogency of the arguments for and against it.

Seventeen

Making Sense of Art and Science

As we have it today, the idea of the public lecture derives from the nineteenth century preoccupation with self-improvement and the promotion of speculative or practical knowledge. As befits that historical origin, such occasions often combine the traditional and the radical: conservative in form, revolutionary in content. I should like to consider two such lectures both given in the same year, each concerned with art and science, and each inclined to compare these two fields of human activity to the disadvantage of the aesthetic side.

George Steiner's 1996 Edinburgh lecture 'A Festival Overture' was widely reported at the time and subsequently much discussed. It posed a serious challenge to the organisers of art festivals in general and to those of the Edinburgh Festival in particular. In it Steiner argued, in effect, that art has had its day and that the area of greatest contemporary creativity, intellectual excitement and human potential is science. His strictures may be well taken against a narrowly expressionist understanding of the nature of art-making; but, as I shall try to show, this conception belongs with certain ideas of subjectivity which draw part of their inspiration from romanticist aesthetic theory. Such a way of thinking is not very old — and, more importantly, nor is it inescapable.

An ancient taxonomy of knowledge established in Greek Antiquity and adopted by philosophers in the later middle ages identifies, as the first division, a distinction between *speculative* or *theoretical* knowledge on the one hand, and *practical* or *technical* knowledge on the other. It is tempting to mark the difference grammatically by distinguishing between 'knowing that' and 'knowing how'. This will not do, however, since *knowing that* using a creamier sauce will produce a more pleasing effect is a matter of practical knowledge whereas *knowing how* the planets move in their orbits is an example of theoretical knowledge.

A better principle, and that deployed by the ancients and the mediaevals, is a teleological or goal-directed one: the different kinds of knowledge are directed towards different *ends* — the speculative towards the *true*, the practical towards the *good*. On this account portrait painting, ship-building, cabinet making and architecture are all examples of practical knowledge. Indeed, since 'art' (L. *ars*; Gk. *techné*) is *skill*, they are all arts. They all aim at one or another kind of practical good. By contrast, pure mathematics, metaphysics and theoretical physics all aim at truths and thus are sciences. Incidentally, this is why theology is sometimes described as sacred science — it aims at the truth about God.

Notice that in this scheme fine art, morality and technology fall under the same general heading. They differ, applying the principle of teleology, according to the kinds of goods to which they are directed. Fine art to the good of pleasure in sight or hearing, morality to the good of virtue in action, and technology to the good of instrumental efficiency. As Aquinas puts it in the *Summa Theologiae*: 'Beauty adds to goodness a relation to the cognitive faculty: so that good means that which simply pleases the appetite; while the beautiful is something pleasant to apprehend'.

Until the modern period this way of thinking was accepted without question and it avoided all sorts of demarcation disputes. Prior to the reception of the renaissance into northern Europe the subsequently diversified roles of builder and architect were unified in the office of the master builder. The skilled draughtsmen who produced the friezes on the walls of gothic chapels were, quite literally, painters and decorators.

By stages, however, and often due to social developments including specialisation and the division of labour, certain distinctions began to emerge between design and implementation, between technology and manufacture, and between art and craft. In the early nineteenth century George Birkbeck, recently qualified in medicine from Edinburgh university, took a job at the fledgling Andersonian Institute in Glasgow. His task was to give lectures in basic science, in chemistry, dynamics and astronomy. To prepare for these he was given an equipment grant in order to modernise the laboratories, and he employed craftsmen ('mechanics') to manufacture new instruments and experimental apparatus. This they were able to do on the basis of copying existing items, but Birkbeck was shocked to discover that they had no idea what the instruments were for. Not only did they lack understanding of scientific theory but their practical skills were detached from any scientific technological knowledge. To his credit Birkbeck established evening classes to make good their deficiencies and so was born the basis of what were to become the Mechanics Institutes, which in turn became major British universities. The Andersonian itself became, by stages, Strathclyde University.

About fifteen years before Birkbeck encountered the mechanics, the Sage of Köningsberg, Immanuel Kant, who along with Scotland's David Hume is reckoned one of the two greatest philosophers of the eighteenth century, sought to complete his own great philosophical system by writing a third 'critique'. The first, the *Critique of Pure Reason* had concerned itself with the structure and preconditions of theoretical knowledge (philosophy, mathematics and science). The second, the *Critique of Practical Reason* was concerned with morality. Notice that the ancients and mediaevals would not have confined an account of practice in this way. Having done so, however, Kant felt the need to provide a critique of another sphere of human life very important in the age of enlightenment, namely the aesthetic. Thus we have the *Critique of Judgement* whose objects of attention are the beautiful and the sublime.

Kant was unquestionably a genius and the third *Critique* is very interesting, proposing an account of aesthetic experience in terms not of its content or special objects but of its formal features including disinterestedness: perception and contemplation apart from any theoretical or practical concern. Nevertheless Kant's detached aesthetic approach did much to legitimise, and in due course to make seem natural, the division between art and applied science; a division which has got in the way of appreciating the creative powers of engineers and experimental scientists to name just two groups which are not normally seen as belonging to any kind of intellectual or cultural elite.

In his 1996 BBC Dimbleby lecture, titled *Science, Delusion and the Appetite for Wonder*, Richard Dawkins initially adopted a positive approach, giving a spirited defence of the intellectual, emotional and aesthetic appeal of science. He observed that Einstein 'was openly ruled by an aesthetic scientific muse' and then quoted him as saying that 'The most beautiful thing we can experience is the mysterious, it is the source of all true art and science'. Einstein is sometimes invoked by avant-garde artists, such as John Latham, who seek the integration of art and science — or the dissolution of the distinction between them. Whether Einstein would himself have favoured this I doubt, but he clearly thought that the two areas of activity arise from the same response to mystery: a mixture of awe and curiosity.

Yet things of common origin may be diverse and even opposed: exploitation and care are conflicting responses to the common perception of the young as vulnerable and unprotected. Similarly one may concede that art and science have a common source while yet wanting to contrast them as ignorance and knowledge, emotion and reason, imagination and discovery, and so on. This is precisely what has happened and what must be countered. Weber spoke of the disenchantment of the world effected by modern science as it stripped the objective order of colours and sounds, meanings and values. Many 'humanists' have responded by denigrating science and elevating non-scientific discourse — especially that pertaining to art.

I share Dawkins's impatience with the posturing relativism of modern cultural theorists; the know-littles who consume educational resources arguing that nothing can be known and then fill what remains of their day celebrating the demise of 'absolutist objectification' and its replacement with 'the aestheticisation of discourse'. That is a waste of time and it brings academic and intellectual life into disrepute. Recognising this, however, is compatible with questioning the scope of science and its adequacy as a comprehensive world-view. In chapter 19 I mention the philosopher Husserl's work *The Crisis of the European Sciences* in which he identifies the modern scientific trend to represent all features of reality in quantitative terms, referring to this as an aspect of the 'mathematisation of nature'. The truth, by contrast, as Husserl emphasised through detailed attention to human experience is that things differ qualitatively as well as quantitatively, and not every true description or explanation is — or can be — couched in scientific terminology.

If 'scientism' is the tendency to treat all questions as either scientific or spurious, then 'artism' is a similarly exclusive habit of viewing all genuine issues as internal to aesthetically-conceived practices. In addition to problems associated with its hegemonic aspirations this condition carries the danger of leading to intellectual autism 'morbid absorption in fantasy'. Scientism risks excluding human experience from the sphere of knowledge, artism denies the category of extra-textual fact. How then to proceed? One response is compatibilism; in effect a form of joint sovereignty. It says there is one world but different ways of conceiving it, and that progress in one way need not be at the cost of another. This is certainly an advance on the plurality of worlds favoured by relativists (my world, your world, he, she and its world, and so on). Compatibilism allows us to say that the flower depicted in a painting is a reality, but that the investigation of its underlying micro-structures and causal processes is the work of molecular biology not art.

This view suggests a division of labour according to subject matter and competence. That in turn implies a basis for mutual respect between art and science and a kind of unity through complementarity. Some artists are influenced by scientific ideas, theories and images; some scientists emphasise the role of the creative imagination in fashioning and expressing their thoughts. Each may learn from the other, but without concluding that the two subjects are really one. In searching for meaning and in trying to make sense one may properly look to the compositional structure and causal relations that constitute the material world but also seek to go beyond these looking for values and purposes intrinsic to human life.

That said, there remains the aspiration to fit our forms of understanding together and thus to construct a map not restricted to this or that region, feature or level, but one that somehow represents the totality. Admittedly it is difficult to see how this might be realised but provided efforts in that direction are alert to, and can resist, the temptation to convert all understanding into a common currency such an ambition should not be discouraged. Who knows? it may lead us to a new renaissance in which, as in the original, poets, artists and scientists work to integrate their insights.

Ironically, Steiner and those whom he criticises share with Dawkins something of the same dubious conception of art. Freed from this exclusively contemplative aesthetic, art takes its place alongside other forms of highly reflective and skilled activity. Rather than see them in opposition it makes more sense to try to bring art and science together. Of course, as ever, one has to avoid facile realisations of this. Giving an art student a video-recorder and a computer no more makes what he or she does good art than does providing a canvas and clay. In fact, much of the video art I have seen is just plain bad. New media take time to master and some prove to be of restricted use. As well as individual experimentation there needs to be shared experience and assessment. This is part of the case for workshops and festivals.

Let there be diversity in festive celebrations of human accomplishment. Let there be music festivals such as Salzburg, visual art festivals like the São Paulo and the Venice Biennale, literary festivals such as Cheltenham, general art festivals and science festivals like those in Edinburgh. But let there also be art *and* science festivals — here the 'and' is not only conjunctive suggesting one thing alongside another, but also indicates a unified subject matter. In contemplating one of these latter festivals Steiner might find reason to rewrite his overture so as to bring it to a more harmonious conclusion, and Dawkins might happily sing along to that tune.

Eighteen

Making Sense of Nature

One of the most striking yet largely unremarked features of contemporary British professional art is its general neglect of landscape. Admittedly there is popular interest in what might be termed 'nature craft', as represented by Andy Goldsworthy and Chris Drury and others. However, this work is object, rather than landscape focused; and whatever its intention its appeal is largely decorative, hence its presentation in coffee-table style publications. The success of Goldsworthy's *Stone* (1994), *Wood* (1998), *Time* (2000), *Passage* (2004) and similar thematic photo-books testifies to public appreciation of inventive crafting with natural materials. A related strand of nature-oriented art is represented by David Nash and Peter Randall-Page. Although more traditionally sculptural in its formalism and in its materials, their work exhibits the same interest in highly aesthetic surfaces, and once again has a greater following outside professional art than within it. Roger Ackling's sun drawings are not well known beyond the art world though they might easily secure wider interest as poetic delicacies, feeding the same appetite for well-crafted artefacts made out of natural materials.

Abstracting from the differences between these artists, one might say that their work celebrates the aesthetic delight of natural forms and textures presented through the medium of middle to small sized objects. In that sense—

though they may not relate themselves to this—it is continuous with certain fashions in craft and gardening. I suspect this fact partly explains the absence of interest in nature among the avant-garde of the last twenty years. For their agendas have been ones of political, cultural and art-institutional analysis and criticism, whose relevant ideas and values stand at some distance from—if not in opposition to— those of domesticated nature craft. The only clear candidate for a new generation artist whose work features landscape, viz. Tania Kovats, has deployed topographical models in the exploration of ideas and images of utopian nature and idealised femininity. In that respect her art is also one of urban cultural commentary, rather than a celebration of nature itself. Accordingly it confirms rather than disrupts the general pattern of neglect of landscape *per se*.

It is all the more interesting, therefore, that the British avant garde of the late 60s and early 70s included artists who turned to nature, landscape and solitary journeying in a spirit of opposition to prevailing art values, and did so without irony. I have in mind particularly Hamish Fulton and Richard Long who are also distinctive in making their walking journeys an essential part of their art.

Aside from the fact that other interests and influences have arisen in the meantime such as feminism, gender theory, post-structuralism, media/music culture, etc., which have no obvious link with the natural world and also engender suspicion of the idea of the natural, and of contemplative detachment, the neglect of landscape may be due to the fact that contemporary artists can see no way of representing it other than by traditional methods, or of otherwise relating themselves to it non-ironically. Against this background it is well worth considering how things could be otherwise, and how they are so in the work of Fulton and Long.

Fulton's first solo exhibition was in 1969 and it introduced a genre that was at once familiar and strange. It was common enough in Britain for a man to don a backpack, go walking, and to take a photograph or two along the way. It was unheard of, however, to claim that the walk was an art form and to suggest that the point of the photographs was to record or to express that activity. Very quickly, however, Fulton attracted critical appreciation. For many, I suspect, the beauty of the black and white images of desolate sky-lines or rough worn pathways was the main focus of inter-est, and Fulton minus photographs would have been hard to envisage let alone enjoy.

By stages, however, the accompanying texts moved up in size and location until they lay across the photographic image; and increasingly there were imageless word pieces. These too grew larger until entire walls were given over to the likes of *rock fall echo dust*. This development was in part an attempt to reassert the claim that the focus of his art was the walk, and to make clear that photographs were not being offered as aesthetically autonomous objects. Put another way, by making works in which words had equal prominence, were dominant, or were exhaustive, he showed that images enjoyed no special privilege in his art.

Richard Long is a contemporary and former fellow student, and developed the central themes, methods and visual forms that that define his work during the same period. Long reintroduced natural landscape as a central theme of art, also making it the location and the material of his sculpture. His earliest work such as *A Line made by walk-ing, England 1967*, exhibited a rare combination of experi-mentation, simplicity and strength. From the mid 1960s, he was creating lines, circles and spirals, walked in grass or dust, inscribed in the earth or laid upon it with sticks or stones. Then there were indoor arrangements of driftwood, pine needles and ever more stones. At first Long worked near to his childhood home in Bristol, then in Ireland and in Scotland, in Europe, in North and South America, in Africa, Australia and Asia. For forty years he has walked and worked, his whole body becoming an instrument for draw-ing upon the earth.

During the period in which he was developing his dis-tinctive forms there were others beginning to work directly on the land, and the use of nature in sculpture has since become familiar. Long respects Fulton with whom he has made occasional walks since their student days in London; but he sees him as different in restricting his work to walks and to texts arising from them—no sculpting or drawing in the landscape. He also sees no real connection with the monumental earth works of Americans Robert Smithson and Michael Heizer, and sees his own art as quite different to that of fellow Briton, Goldsworthy. All Long says about the relationship between his own innovations and later 'nature art' is 'If one person opens the door others can walk through'.

In fact there is a wide gulf between the unsentimental visionary realism of Long who is happiest with wilderness and intimations of infinity, and the more rural, intimate and decorative craftwork of Goldsworthy. Long has no desire for his art to shock, unsettle, disturb or even puzzle viewers. But nor is it meant to be a source of comfort or nostalgia for city dwellers. One recent work featured a phrase heard in Ireland 'This global warming seems to be doing us some good'. Was he quoting this ironically? His answer will surprise and even disappoint some of his admirers:

> I started making my work in the 1960s for completely different reasons from green politics. It is not part of an environmental manifesto; it's not evangelical or political; it's about art. I do care about nature and the environment. In specific cases if we can do something we should and I have supported particular projects and campaigns. But that doesn't mean that we should think that all change is a bad thing. There will always be change. It is part of the very nature and life of the planet.

Given his engagement with nature, the global range of his travels, and his use of the ready-to-hand, it might be thought inevitable that Long's work would have transcended the culturally local, achieving a form of art-making that seems universal in its aims, elements and methods. Yet it could easily have gone wrong. The relationship with nature could have become ideological, clichéd or precious. The journeying could have degenerated into a form of cultural tourism, or pious ritual. The use of natural materials might so easily have descended to the level of rustic decoration. In fact, he has grown in strength as an artist, presenting an original vision aided by a fertile imagination, and a refined sensibility. Strong ideas, rooted in unsentimental engagements with the world.

Likewise any tendency to view his work as visually pleasing but intellectually unsophisticated is challenged by an early photographic piece: *England* (1967), which shows an upright rectangular frame standing in the foreground, through which can be seen in the distance a white circle on a hill side. I used to think of this in relation to earlier English paintings of ancient hill drawings, as by Paul Nash and Eric Ravillious, and also as signalling Long's farewell to depicted forms and his move to directly inscribing them on the surface of the earth. In fact, however, it is an exploration of the relativity of locations and objects to the standpoint of the observer.

Long does what he chooses, not seeking to challenge or subvert viewers but equally not seeking to impress or charm them. There is an ongoing oscillation between the sensible and the intelligible, the sensuous and the rational. They are sometimes conjoined but are never altogether disjoined. His work is always particular. No item could be substituted for any other as serving the same general purpose. There are no general purposes for Long: everything is singular. His work adds to the world and changes our perception of it; evidently it also answers to a desire to relate to natural landscape. 'People need art,' he says,

> it raises the spirits. It's also a big part of what makes us human; it's part of our fundamental identity: people need to make art and people want to see it. I want to do all of these things but I also want to communicate through what I make, so that years later the ideas will still be there for others to see and understand.

The neglect of landscape in British art is a result in part of the process of urbanisation, which has led to most artists being raised in town and city environments and conforming to prevalent ideals of ironic sophistication, social know-ingness and sensationalism. From that perspective nature is generally seen either as a place of occasional recreation or as an 'issue' to be commented upon and perhaps campaigned about. What it is not is a place or state in which to go in search of understanding human nature and its fulfilment. Yet there is a recurrent tendency in British art since the period of the industrial revolution, marked by such figures as Constable, Linnell, Palmer, Blake, Nash, Sutherland, Hitchens, Long and Fulton, in which highly individual art-ists react against layered artifice and ironic social commen-tary to engage directly with places and conditions which for the greater part of our history provided our habitation and occupations. In working and seeking meaning in the natu-ral landscape they have also been engaged in a kind of archeological recovery of what lies beneath the surface of even the most urban environment. Little wonder, then, that their work seems at once both strange and familiar.[1]

---

[1]   For images of work by Hamish Fulton and Richard Long, see, respectively: www.hamish-fulton.com, and www.richardlong.com

Nineteen

Finding Meaning In Enchantment

Quoting a phrase of the poet and philosopher Friedrich Schiller, Max Weber famously wrote of 'the disenchantment of the world' effected by the rise of modern science. Part of that disenchantment came with the substitution of quantity for quality as the index of difference. For the ancients and the mediaevals, things, places and times were the loci of natures and essences. Of each thing one might ask *quid est?* (what is it?) and hope to have this answered by a specification of its *quiddity* (its what-it-is-ness). This pre-modern view also included the idea that nature is dynamic and purposeful: *agere sequitur esse* — acting follows upon being, or, equivalently, as a thing is so it acts.

Thus, to understand the quiddity of an object was to see it as an agent in process of realising its nature. An egg is not just a quantity of viscous liquid, but the instantiation of a specific essence on its way to being a bird; and a child is a human being on its way to adulthood, and thence onward to heaven, purgatory or hell.

In time, however, mediaeval Aristotelianism gave way to Descartes' geometry of volumes and to the science of measurement. In obvious ways innovatory, this also represented a return to the old philosophy of the Greek atomists: all things are but aggregations of particles in the void, and all qualitative differences are but appearances resulting from quantitative and combinatory variation. In his book

The Crisis of the European Sciences, the Austrian philosopher and founder of phenomenology Edmund Husserl captured this change when he wrote of 'the mathematisation of nature'.

The world mathematised and disenchanted still offers something to the artistic imagination, but the art inspired by the scientific view is, of necessity, silent on the very things that animate our experience: the sense of self and of other, of love and of loss, of memory and of anticipation. Seen from the perspective of the atoms and of their smaller constituents, these are transient wisps, vaporous by-products of particles in motion. Whatever the truth about the relationship between matter and mind, however, it is mind that matters. So far as meaning and value are concerned, to be is to be experienced. Hence any art that aims to make sense of these features must of necessity be phenomenological: an aesthetic exploration of felt qualitative differences, and of perceived significance.

These philosophical thoughts were occasioned by looking at some thirty paintings in the R.W. Norton Art Gallery in Shreveport, Louisiana. Just over the border from northeast Texas and south of Arkansas, in both of which states gaming is illegal, Shreveport has become something of a gambling town. A growing cluster of casino-hotels and riverboats provide for the spirited and digestive parts, while businesses such as the *Peace of Mind Center* offer 'instinctive and astrological readings, massage and aromatherapy'. To judge from the size of the (dining) tables at the Epic Buffet in the *Hollywood Casino*, and by the generations gathered at them, the casino restaurants are more 'eat all you can' happy diners than they are gamblers' refuelling stops.

Midway between the downtown casinos and the airport lies an area that owes its wealth to the pre-gambling oil economy. Thereabouts, amid woodland and azalea gardens stands the Norton Gallery. In the early 1930s Richard Norton and others discovered the Rodessa oil field in north Louisiana. After his death, his son and widow used their wealth to establish an art foundation, and twenty years later the Gallery opened to the public. The dominant theme is the romance of America. The Old West frontier is celebrated in cowboy and Indian paintings (and sculptures) by Frederic Remington and Charles Russell. Colt 45s, Winchester specials and the like, gilded and engraved, fill the Antique Firearms section; and elsewhere the Civil War leaders of the Southern States are honoured in the Confederate Gallery.

The last of these displays begins to move the mind from thoughts of physical endeavour to intimations of romantic melancholy and nostalgia for a lost world. Herein enters Felix Kelly, the New Zealand born painter whose highly evocative scenes of the South I had come five thousand miles to see. Kelly died in 1994 at the age of eighty. Once heralded by Herbert Read as 'a poet of the inner court', Kelly was little known other than to those owners of country houses, manors, and neo-classical villas in England and the US who commissioned him to paint their homes, as much for future generations as for themselves. So far did he enter into the world of country houses, and so considerable became his knowledge of their architecture that he made a series of paintings on the theme of Palladio's Villa Capra, or Rotunda, which formed the basis for an architectural scheme. This was commissioned by Sebastian de Ferranti and implemented by Julian Bicknell at Henbury Hall at Macclesfield in the north of England. Kelly was also involved in the restoration of Castle Howard and of Highgrove, the Prince of Wales's Gloucestershire residence.

Born in Auckland in 1914, Felix Kelly came to London in 1935, and four years later joined the RAF. A self-taught artist, he began to work in London as a commercial designer and cartoonist, the latter principally for *Lilliput* magazine, and signing himself 'Fix'. Later he used the period of his war service to develop his talents as a painter. In 1943 he had a show at the Reid and Lefevre Gallery in St James's, and the following year exhibited there again in a group show along with Lucian Freud and Julian Trevelyan. It was around this time that Read developed an interest in his quasi-surrealist work, commissioning half-a-dozen paintings to be used as illustrations for his novel *The Green Child* (1945). In the year after its publication the Falcon Press included these along with some thirty five other images in *Paintings by Felix Kelly*, to which Read contributed a short but laudatory and perceptive introduction. Having noted Kelly's habit of adding some imaginative element to his depiction of English country houses Read continues: 'Not content with such an obtrusive romantic accent in an otherwise realistic record, Felix Kelly abandon the limits of nature's topography and invents the landscapes of a dream world'. That style of invention later led him into stage design beginning with a commission from John Geilgud to produce the sets for his production of *A Day by the Sea* at the Haymarket in London in the early 1950s.

I first came across Kelly's work in the form of a lithograph made around the same time as the publication of the Falcon Press book. This was his contribution to the 'School Prints' series commissioned after the war and produced by the Baynard Press for distribution to British schools. The noble motive, conceived by Brenda Rawnsley, was to enliven and inspire a generation of children growing up in rubbled and rationed austerity; and, as she wrote to artists in her letter of commission, '[to give] school-children an idea of contemporary art'. Materially reduced they might be, but aesthetically deprived they need not be. The project was very much in the spirit of Herbert Read's conviction that art could improve the child by developing his or her imagination. Read was chairman of the selection committee for *School Prints*, and I suspect that he played a role in Kelly's being included in among the artists invited to contribute.

Kelly's lithograph, *Drifter and Paddle Steamers* (1946), illustrations of which appear on the cover of this book, recalls the work of Eric Ravilious. Muted colours in close tonal harmonies suggest a mistiness, which combined with a drawing style that is more schematic than observational, creates a dream world of satisfying simplicity. The white cliffs, calm channel and model-like tall funnelled boats are far removed from the ravages of war, and even from the wear, tear and flux of everyday existence. But the key in which the theme of untroubled life is played is not so much nostalgic as enchanted.

This description will mislead if it is taken to suggest a world in which things do, or might, happen contrary to nature; or at least contrary to the laws that govern the course of things in the actual world. Kelly's vision is quasi-mystical. The world he depicts is ours but not as we have become accustomed to seeing it. By amplifying, selecting and re-setting he effects not fantasy but re-enchantment. The essence of the world is as it appears: a natural theatre in which narratives are played out by generation upon generation of actors.

This aspect becomes clearer in works in which Kelly's technique and subject matter overlap with those of Edward Wadsworth and Tristram Hillier. They too were in search of meaning and found it in the calm depiction of places where the natural and human worlds meet: in farming landscapes, in train-traversed woodlands, and in harbour and shore scenes. Here nature is shown to be providential; land and sea yield to human need and the evidence of cultivation, construction and harvest stand like figures on a stage. One common theme, and one which links them to continental European paintings of the same period is the positioning of artefacts in open air still lives. Typically items related to the setting, such as boats, anchors, markers and buoys, arranged on the shore, stand both as well-balanced elements in an orderly still-life and as personae on a stage. The echoes of surrealism are audible but the greater resonance is with the Italian metaphysical painters including De Chirico and Morandi.

There is, though, even greater restraint in these English artists, moving them yet further from fantasy towards realism. Ravilious was once widely known and Wadsworth has received a degree of critical attention, but Hillier is now largely forgotten and Kelly seems never to have been discussed in print other than by one or two enthusiasts such as Read initially, and then Robert Harling (sometime architectural correspondent of the *Sunday Times* and subsequently editor of *House and Garden*) who was most enamoured by Kelly's studies of houses, real and imagined. The general critical neglect is ill-deserved, for these were artists of tender sensibilities and visionary imaginations whose work both rewards meditative attention and could serve as inspiration for a new generation of poetic landscape painters.

So far as broad critical appreciation is concerned, Kelly may have been a victim of his own success. Evidently his romanticism and feel for historic houses and their settings secured him commissions and a following among the well-to-do of the English counties. While these include some very discerning collectors, their tastes on the whole favour the conventional and are directed towards paintings as furnishings, and as forms of family documentation. As Read remarked, 'he paints for the "cabinet", for the intimate world of people who surround themselves with private possessions rather than artefacts of culture'. Here Kelly's visions may have seemed more charming than challenging; and his paintings show an increasing tendency towards the decorative which ill serves the case for taking him as a serious artist of ideas. This criticism may be somewhat anachronistic, however; and the argument can be made that his work was never merely ornamental.

Given the lamentable shortage of paintings on public display (the Norton being the sole exception, I know of) it is hard to be sure about the course of his development. My sense, however, is that he moved from a youthful infatuation with the romantic ruins of an England past, through a poetic-cum-philosophical interest in a timeless England that lies beneath the surface of apparent change, to a fascination with the Southern States of the US and later with then remoter parts of the world such as Russia, India and Thailand where he found buildings and ambient landscapes that spoke of forms of life that possessed (and expressed) an expansive and coherent meaning. These further travels also provided opportunities for foreign commissions: in the late

1960s, for example, he produced a large scale study of the Himalayas for the King of Nepal.

The Norton Gallery has twenty-two Kellys on display, most contained within a space dedicated to him. Painted on board, with fine brushwork and to a high finish, the main pieces are partly reminiscent of Dutch landscapes. The composition, colour and light owe something to van Ruisdael, and much of the subject matter is in the classical tradition of Palladia in Arcadia; but the particulars are unique to Kelly. Mansions stand proud on the edge of the bayou or atop dramatic cliffs. Persons, real, notional, or ghostly provide links to nature and to the spectator as they look out upon the landscape or towards the viewer. Moments are captured in meditation by them and by us, and such themes as love and loss, companionship and loneliness, labour and recreation, float to the surface of one's attention.

In one of a pair of paintings executed in 1976, *Coastal Railroad* a rocky leg twists up and out of the sea, while to the left a wooden-carriaged train arcs towards the viewer; the whole scene appearing through the frame of a veranda shaded by a pink-striped awning. The immediate subject is the gracious world of the old South, but this in turn stands for a set of more general values: civility, gentility, and the harmonious integration of man and nature. All of this being mediated by buildings whose design and location embodies those very same values.

Kelly painted what Edmund Burke articulated in prose: the virtues of traditional conservatism. In part philosophy, in part sensibility, this celebrates the ownership and cultivation of the land and the maintenance of good order, not so much through the imposition of rules, as through the development of personal habits of care and respect. Burke fashioned his ideas in a period when France had undergone a revolution and when the American colonies had rebelled against British rule. His concern was that abstract principles of justice could not serve so well the interests of the individual and the community as could settled habits of action and avoidance. In this his philosophy was akin to that of his contemporary Dr Johnson. It was apt, therefore, that in the 1970s Kelly was commissioned by Harvard to paint a series of roundels showing scenes from Johnson's life for installation in the ceiling of the University's Houghton Library.

The Burkean philosophy had its strong adherents in America's Old South and still today something of that agrarian conservatism survives. Perhaps this is what attracted Kelly, an erstwhile colonial, to rural Louisiana and Alabama. There he could find the remains of an older European order in which the implicit metaphysics of the ancient and medieval worlds found expression. But he also shows signs of its passing in architectural ruination and in the vegetation that crawls over it. Kelly would surely have loved the paddle steamers that worked the Red River in earlier times; but it is hard to believe that he could have viewed the new casino boats in Shreveport with equal pleasure, and I doubt that he would have lunched at the Epic Buffet. Times change but Kelly's paintings help one to see that, in parts at least, the world remains a place of enchantment.

Twenty

Journey's End

My general title refers to 'seeking meaning and making sense'. Evidently one may seek something without finding it; but to speak of 'making sense' suggests an achievement, and in the context of the search for meaning it further suggests a successful quest. Leaving aside the question of whatever successes or failures may be represented by the preceding chapters, I wish to conclude by reflecting on an ambiguity in the expression 'making sense' which conveniently presents us with two contrasting attitudes to the whole question of whether there is any such thing as *meaning* in the various departments of human thought and practice, and if there is, what it may amount to. For we may think of 'making sense' as a *discovery* of what is there already, some intrinsic order of intelligibility, purpose or value, waiting to be made sense of; or we may think of the process as being one of *construction*, of making sense as one might make a picture or make (up) a story.

In the opening chapter 'In Search of Meaning' I considered the criticism common among postmodernists that traditional notions of meaning and value, provided by religious narratives or by philosophical theories of human nature, are no longer tenable since they rest on false beliefs in objective metaphysical and natural realities. For these critics, I said, 'searching for meaning in life is like hunting for unicorns — both are pointless activities based on empty myths'. I then noted three styles of response to such subversive scepticism or nihilism: first, *romantic reaffirmation*, second, *self-conscious irony*, and third, *reform and renewal*. I favour the last of these, rearticulating and where necessary amending older conceptions of human nature and human values so as to show their coherence, plausibility and contemporary relevance. The preceding chapters have born upon that task by considering particular examples of practices of reasoning and making sense; but as I noted earlier there is a second way of vindicating traditional ideas, namely by showing that they have a part in our best understanding of human experience at a very general level — and not a mere walk-on contribution, or even a small speaking part, but a central and indispensable role in the human story.

The sceptic or nihilist may respond that it is one thing to find that human beings recurrently resort to certain styles of thought and evaluation, and quite another for those to be coherent, let alone justified. After all, it is a familiar theme of subversive criticism that what proclaims itself as rational is in fact a pathological search for security, and what asserts itself as good is in truth a strategy for exercising domination. Arresting as these suggestions may appear, such criticisms are themselves open to just the same analysis. Might not the postmodernist be asserting the absence of truth and of value out of a fear that if they exist then he or she will be under the burden of recognising and respecting them? Might not the denial of a religious reality be an expression of fear lest there be a standpoint of judgement beyond human prejudice, and a prospect of eternal gain or loss? These are serious matters to contemplate, and it would not be a surprise if rather than face them inventive people devised the coping strategy of saying that after all they are only fearful fictions.

Moreover, there is second-order consideration which suggests that where a style of thinking, and its associated presuppositions, are recurrent and even constitutive of areas of thought and practice that are otherwise found to be valid and productive, then the indispensability of those presuppositions may be the best argument there is for believing in them. Consider, for example the practice of arbitrating competing claims, or that of imposing sanctions for misconduct. In the course of these, assertions may be made about what is fair or fitting, and these may themselves be contested by appeal to the idea of justice, either that dispensed by a higher authority, or ultimately that of justice itself. The subversive critic may then suggest that talk of fairness and of fittingness is simply a veiled invocation of power or interest. Taking that prospect seriously, however, does not eliminate the possibility that there is right and wrong in the matter. Someone may assert that justice requires such and such, out of a motive of greed or fear, and institutions may perhaps be created for the same reason; but it seems impossible not to think that these very facts require us to ask whether the verdicts and sanctions were then themselves unjust. Indeed, the natural, if not the logical implication of a claim to ulterior motive is that the action in question was wrong.

Of course it may not be: a mathematical calculation done out of a wish to impress rather than out a concern for truth, may nonetheless be correct; and a verdict handed down and a sanction imposed out of a wish to dominate may nonetheless be in accord with abstract principles of impartial justice. Not only that, but the latter promise answers to a question that will not go away: was what was done, in itself right? It is imaginable that we might be so innocent as not to wonder about possible ulterior motives in the dispensation of 'justice'. It is inconceivable that we could have arbitration and the administration of sanctions without the question arising: is this fair? This is simply part of the human form of life.

'Well it may be' concedes the critic, but that does not show that there is any such thing as justice *per se*, or equivalently, that there are truths about what justice (the principle not some particular institution) requires. Now, however, we are entitled to ask where lies the standpoint which the critic occupies and which is outside the human form of life. This is, of course, an ironical question intended to make the point that our *judgements* about what is the case are and can only be *our* judgements, informed by what we know, or believe we know—from small detail to general structure. And what we believe we know, as evidenced by what we say and do, and by how we evaluate what others say and do, is that there is truth and falsity, there is virtue and vice, there is justice and injustice, there is beauty and ugliness, there is nobility and depravity, and there is reverence and blasphemy. This being so, there is also the question, now an unambiguously philosophical one, of what all of this implies about the nature of reality.

The unsubtle critic having been given something to think about, if not being altogether dispensed with, there is a more nuanced questioner to be addressed. This person agrees that human experience is structured by meanings and values, and further agrees that this fact cannot be set aside by positing alternative explanations of why we think in these terms, and therefore accepts that we are, and are set to remain meaning and value governed beings. Yet he nonetheless withholds assent to meaning and value as objective realities. This subtle doubter acknowledges that we are meaning-seeking and sense-making beings, recognises that sense-making is not the same as asserting power or attempting to resist death, but yet thinks that making sense is not a matter of discovery but one of construction or invention. On this account we are indeed answerable to standards of value and virtue, and are aesthetic and even spiritual beings; but we are all of these to the extent that, and because, we are imaginative and creative animals that construct an intermediate surface between ourselves and the purely material world, an intermediary lining on which we draw and colour our compositions.

This is a concession to objectivity, allowing that there is something we seem to see which calls for our attention and earns our regard, but it is also and fundamentally a form of subjectivism inasmuch as it regards the source of that 'something' as lying within us. By way of illustration of what I have in mind consider the following from Roger Scruton, unquestionably the most important British writer on aesthetics, and a brilliant practitioner of the art of illuminating the structure of human meanings:

> 'Birth, copulation and death are the moments when time stands still, when we look on the world from a point at its edge, when we experience our dependence and contingency, and when we are apt to be filled with an entirely reasonable awe. It is from such moments, replete with emotional knowledge, that religion begins, and the rational person is not the one who scoffs at all religions, but the one who tries to discover which of them, if any, can make sense of those things, and, while doing so, draw the poison of resentment ('The Sacred and the Human', *Prospect*, August 2007).

Admittedly this is a kind of psychologising, but not one that seeks to subvert the dimension of human experience that it describes. It is rather an exercise in reflexive 'natural history', noting that this is a part of the human (i.e. our) form of life, and explaining what is going on within it in terms borrowed from the relevant sensibility and practices themselves. Be it respectful, however, it remains a challenge to the realist interpretation in which human practices are contrasted with transcendent realities. There seem, then, to be three positions in contest: the subversive *sceptic-cum-nihilist* who says it is all a meaningless projection; the *hermeneutic constructivist* who recognises the dimension of meaning as having its own structure and hierarchy of values; and the *value realist* who urges that what is rejected *tout court* by the former, and is recognised by the latter, however partially, is something real and unconstructed.

How to resolve the dispute between the second and third parties? In the year following the end of World War I, the political theorist and economist Harold Laski wrote as follows:

> … Our business if we desire to live a life not utterly devoid of meaning and significance, is to accept nothing which contradicts our basic experience merely because it comes to us from tradition or convention or authority. It may well be that we shall be wrong; but our self-expression is thwarted at the root unless the certainties we are asked to accept coincide with the certainties we experience. That is why the

condition of freedom in any state is always a widespread
and consistent skepticism of the canons upon which power
insists. ('The Dangers of Obedience', *Harper's Monthly
Magazine*, Vol. 159 (1919)).

Laski was writing about a political situation, in a time of
post-war trauma, in the wake of the Russian Revolution,
and from the perspective of a socialist intent upon creating a
more just society. His socialism, however, owed more to
nineteenth century British moral thinkers, in particular
John Stuart Mill, than to Marx and Engels. Here Laski
adopts a familiar revolutionary theme, namely the attack
upon tradition, convention or authority; but the real target
of his concern seems to be inauthenticity. The reason for
questioning established ideas is not that they may be
wrong, or even that they are promulgated from on high, but
that if we are to be self-expressing creatures then whatever
we give life to must originate within, or at least be confirmed from that quarter. Scepticism here is not directed
against the possibility of objective truth handed down to us
but suggests that our own avowals may be inauthentic, not
issuing from our own certainties but from those of others
which we then unquestioningly accept.

This theme was once very familiar, being frequently
voiced by progressives — particularly in the spheres of
education. It is, though, flawed in two respects. First the
elevation of personal experience over other sources of
knowledge is a residue of empiricism, i.e. of the belief that
all true knowledge has to be traceable to the impact of the
world upon one's own senses. The reality, however, is that
before we are in a position to validate propositions against
experience we must first be able to formulate them, and that
calls for conceptual resources that were acquired in the process of being taught a language, and which were deployed
in experience long before we were able to adopt a critical
perspective upon it. In short our ability to question authority itself depends upon authoritative instruction that,
logically, we could not have questioned.

Second, Laski's highlighting of the themes of scepticism and certainty suggests the application of a misapplied standard to external sources, which, they having failed it, are then substituted for by internal conviction. In other words, Laski agrees with what he takes to be the proper demand of certainty, but because of his empiricism he relocates this internally, within the individual subject. Later thinkers, having learned the lesson of the many attacks on the very idea of objective certainty, then take the further step of concluding that the only way in which something could enjoy authority is if it were beyond questioning by the subject; and the only way in which this possibility could be provided for is if the subject is his own authority in virtue of having created the thing in question. We can only find meaning and make sense if we are ourselves the authors of meaning and the constructors of sense.

Given this diagnosis a remedy suggests itself. If you agree that seeking meaning and making sense are part of the human form of life, and if your reason for not allowing that these activities could have objective counterparts is that we could never be certain of having identified them unless they were our own creations, then let go of the demand of certainty. Making sense is a fallible business, and just like any other human endeavour that seeks to align itself with objective standards there is no reason to think that a first-person perspective is more likely to be right than an external guide. Seeking meaning is something that human beings do, as is making sense. It is hard even to describe these activities without presupposing objective standards for them; and an acceptance of human fallibility and of our dependence on the authority of others releases us from the pressure to protect the idea of making sense by treating it as a matter of construction (about which we cannot be accused of error), rather than one of discovery (with the implication that we may fail). Interestingly, therefore, the most intellectually modest position is the realist one. It postulates a destination without assuming that we are on the right road towards it, or that having set out we must arrive. The corollary of this modesty, however, is the prospect that if we reach journey's end in the search for meaning then we will indeed be able to make sense of things by having discovered real truths about human life and its fulfilment.

Index